# THE BAYREUTH LETTERS

OF

# RICHARD WAGNER

# THE STORY OF BAYREUTH

## AS TOLD IN

# THE BAYREUTH LETTERS

## OF

# RICHARD WAGNER

TRANSLATED AND EDITED BY
CAROLINE V. KERR

*Illustrated from Photographs*

SCIRE · QVOD
SCIENDVM

NEW YORK
VIENNA HOUSE
1972

Originally published by Small, Maynard and Company
Boston, 1912


First Vienna House edition published 1972

International Standard Book Number:
0-8443-0015-2


Library of Congress Catalogue Card Number: 78-163795


*Manufactured in the United States of America*

# CONTENTS

# ILLUSTRATIONS

# THE ORIGIN AND DEVELOPMENT
## OF THE
## BAYREUTH FESTIVAL IDEA

In order to be able to see the life work of Richard Wagner in its true perspective it is necessary always to keep in mind *Bayreuth*, where the spirit of the great composer is ever revived by fresh artistic deeds.

"Richard Wagner in Bayreuth" — the master and his life work — is the only proper and comprehensive formula by which to measure the events which took place here.

Richard Wagner is an art phenomenon which it would be as difficult to explain away as a Beethoven, a Goethe, or a Schiller.

It is to the latter that he is the most clearly related; he is the musical counterpart of the "greatest German of them all," whose art, like Wagner's, sent its roots down deep into German national feeling and character.

It was this intense longing to " nationalise " his art which gave Wagner the incomparable energy necessary for creating a home for his life work, where it would live and thrive in its essential purity.

Bayreuth, then, is not only the little Bavarian city which furnished a local habitation and a name for the Wagnerian music drama, but it is also the embodiment of an idea which reaches back more than a quarter of a century in the life of the composer.

As early as 1848, during his official connection with the Royal Opera in Dresden, Wagner wrote a feuilleton on a " Project for the Organisation of a German National Theatre," in which he made a plea for fewer performances, but these to be of a superior quality, and he gave excellent and practical advice for the realisation of such a project.

He breaks a lance for the same idea in his treatise on " The Theatre in Zurich " (1851), " The Vienna Royal Opera " (1863), and a

"German National School of Music" (1863), which he hoped to be able to found in Munich.

The real germ of the idea, however, which was to crystallise eventually into the Bayreuth Festival of 1876, is indissolubly connected with the creation of the heroic tetralogy "Ring of the Nibelung."

To his friend, Friedrich Heine, he wrote, in 1850, the half-jesting, half-prophetic lines:

"I am now thinking of writing the music to 'Siegfried.' In order to be able to produce it properly some day, I am cherishing all sorts of bold and unusual plans, for the realisation of which nothing further is necessary than that some rich old uncle or other should take it into his head to die."

Writing in a more serious strain to Uhlig, he amplifies the idea, and presents its details so clearly as to leave no room for doubt as to the powerful hold it has taken upon his heart and mind. The tempting sum of five hundred thalers had, at the instigation of Franz Liszt, been offered for his " Siegfried " by the ducal theatre at Weimar. Referring to this, he writes:

" I should like to send ' Siegfried ' into the world in a different fashion from that which would be possible to the good people of Weimar. With this in mind, I am occupied with plans which appear chimerical at the first glance, and yet it is this alone which gives me courage to finish ' Siegfried.' In order to carry into execution my plans in regard to the best, the most important and significant work which I am able to produce under any circumstances, — in short to accomplish the conscious mission of my life, — would mean a matter of ten thousand thalers.

" If I could command such a sum, I should proceed as follows:

" Here, in Zurich, where I now chance to be, and where many conditions are far from unfavourable, I should erect a rough theatre of planks and beams, according to my own plans, in a beautiful meadow near the city, and furnish it merely with the scenery and machinery necessary for 'Siegfried.' Then I would select the best available artists and invite them to come to Zurich. I should go about securing my orchestra in the same way. At the New Year a notification of the event would be made through the leading newspapers of Germany to all friends of the musical drama, with an invitation to be present at the proposed musical Festival; anyone giving due notice and coming to Zurich for the purpose would be assured of admission, gratis of course, as would be all admissions.

" The invitation would be further extended to the young people of Zurich, the University students, and members of the various choral unions.

" When everything was in order, I should give three performances of 'Siegfried' in the course of a week; after the third, the theatre would be pulled down and the score burned.

" To those people who had been pleased with the thing, I should say, ' Now let me see you do the same!'

" If, however, they wished to hear something

more from my pen, I should say, ' You furnish the money!'

"Well, do I seem quite mad to you! It may be, but I assure you that to be able to do this is the end and aim of my life, and the only prospect which could tempt me to commence a new work of art.

"So now! get me ten thousand thalers! That is all I ask of you!"

Rather than interfere with the realisation of this as yet visionary plan for a monumental performance of the complete work, Franz Liszt magnanimously relinquished his idea of standing sponsor to the "Siegfried" music drama, as he had for "Lohengrin" in 1850, although the first performance of the work had virtually been promised him by a letter written by Wagner in 1852, in which he said:

"I can only imagine my audience as being composed of friends who have assembled in some place for the purpose of becoming acquainted with my works — preferably, in some beautiful retreat far from the smoke and industrial odours of city civilisation; as such a retreat, I should at the most consider Weimar, but certainly no larger city." . . .

The following prefatory remarks appeared in connection with the first edition of the drama of the " Ring of the Nibelung," which appeared in 1862:

" With me the chief thing is to imagine such a performance as entirely free from the influence of the repertory system in vogue in our permanent theatres. Accordingly, I have in mind one of the smaller German cities, favourably located and adapted to the entertainment of distinguished guests, and particularly a city in which there would be no collision with a larger permanent theatre, and where, consequently, a strictly metropolitan theatrical public with its well-known customs would not present itself. Here a provisionary theatre would be erected, as simple as possible, perhaps only of wood, and with the interior only designed for artistic purposes. I should confer with an experienced and intelligent architect as to a plan for such a house, with ample theatrical arrangements of the seats, and the decided advantage of an invisible orchestra. Here then, in the early spring months, the leading dramatic singers, chosen from the *ensemble* of the German opera houses, would be assembled, in order to study the various parts of my stage work, entirely uninterrupted by any other claims upon their artistic activity.

" On the days appointed for the performance — of which I have in mind three in all — the German public would be invited to be present, as these performances, like those of our large music festivals, are to be made accessible, not only to the partial public of any one city, but to all friends of art, far and near.

" A complete performance of the dramatic poem in question would take place in midsummer — on a fore-evening ' Das Rheingold,' and on the three following evenings the chief dramas ' Die Walküre,' ' Siegfried,' and ' Götterdämmerung.' "

After discussing at length, the advantages which would accrue to the artists by " concentrating all their intellectual powers upon one style and one task," Wagner takes up the question of the invisible orchestra:

" To complete the impression of such a performance, I should lay great stress upon an invisible orchestra, which it would be possible to effect by the architectural illusion of an amphitheatrical arrangement of the auditorium.

" The importance of this will be clear to anyone who attends our present operatic performances for the purpose of gaining any genuine impression of the dramatic art work, and finds himself made the involuntary witness of the technical evolutions caused by the unavoidable view of the mechanical movements made by the musicians and their leader. These should be as carefully concealed as the wires, roped canvas, and boards of the stage machinery, the sight of which, as everyone knows, creates a most disturbing impression and one calculated to destroy all illusions.

" After having experienced what a pure, ethe-realised tone the orchestra gains by being heard through an acoustic sounding-board which has the effect of eliminating all the indispensable but non-musical sounds which the instrumentalist is obliged to make in producing the tone; and after having realised the advantageous position in which the singer is placed to his listeners, by being able to stand, as it were, directly before them — no one could arrive at other than a favourable conclusion as to the effectiveness of my plan for an acoustic-architectural arrange-ment." . . .

In all the excerpts it is easy to trace the germinative idea of the Bayreuth Festival in its evolution and eventual characteristics.

There we have a special festival stage, erected far from the noise and bustle of the metropolis, an invisible orchestra, a band of chosen artists, — fully in sympathy with the task intrusted to them, — an audience assembled for the sake of the art work, a summer season, and a biennial repetition.

Wagner projected these ideas with that fine free breadth which characterises the mind of genius, but the " three full years " which he allowed himself for the completion of his heroic musical task — " Ring of the Nibelung " — became, in reality, a quarter of a century filled with struggles and disappointments, baffling to anyone but a reformer fighting for an idea which embodied his " conscious mission in life."

Having seen how the idea of a special festival for the correct and adequate performance of his tetralogy had become an obsession with Wagner, we are now to follow it through its evolution and ultimate realisation in the so-called " Bayreuth Letters."

.     .     .     .     .     .     .

This correspondence, addressed to four of his most faithful henchmen, furnishes a clear and sustained story of the five years preceding the first Bayreuth Festival, told in the authentic words of its creator.

Shortly before his death in Venice (February

13, 1883) Wagner wrote to Friedrich Feustel, one of the loyal fellow workers mentioned above, a few lines which might aptly serve as a motto for this book:

" When I take a general survey of the attitude of my own age to me during the past ten years, I must confess that the balance of my gratitude falls on the side of the friends I made during that time, and I herewith declare that, next to my family, the dearest of all things to me is Bayreuth."

In another place he writes:

" I should have given up the entire undertaking had I given up Bayreuth. So far as my great Festival Play has as yet attracted attention, it is inseparably associated with the name of Bayreuth."

Of the friends whose services are perpetuated in the " Bayreuth Letters," four take a conspicuous position by reason of their personal activity in the various preparatory phases of the epoch-making Festival. These four helpers —

Friedrich Feustel, Theodor Muncker, Emil Heckel, and Carl Brandt — were German to the core, and especially well suited to fight for the realisation of the great German art work of the future.

Glasenapp has given us admirable pen portraits of these four men in his " Life of Richard Wagner," and from this I quote in free translation:

" Feustel was actively occupied with political matters connected both with the German Empire and his own city of Bayreuth, and enjoyed a position of great confidence among his fellow citizens. His sense of justice, his keenness of vision, and his financial instincts, which made him so valuable a citizen, also fitted him exceptionally for effective work in connection with the great art reformation planned by Wagner. His entire strength, business ability, untiring energy, and knowledge of worldly affairs were placed at the service of the Bayreuth Idea. . . .

" He was the propelling personality; for when

Muncker held back and cautioned economy, Feustel pushed aggressively forward. He was not at all disposed to sit with folded hands and await the development of events, but to attack and overcome the obstacles which presented themselves.

"He was always *en route*, and could in this way do much for the cause; the manner in which he was given to eliminating space provoked Wagner to call him familiarly 'The Flying Dutchman of Bayreuth.'"

In summing up the characteristics of Theodor Muncker, the burgomaster of Bayreuth, Glasenapp makes use of the following tribute, in which a son does honour to a father's memory:

"There was certainly much in Wagner's thoughts and work which lay beyond my father's intellectual sphere. He was lacking in the formal philosophical schooling and the scientific knowledge necessary for grasping clearly the magnitude of the individual Wagnerian works. But that which he could not analyse with logical acumen he accepted in a purely naïve sense, and

viewed them in their entirety as they mirrored
themselves in the bottom of his soul. With the
heart, more than with the head, he comprehended
Wagner the artist and philosophic thinker, and
the most devoted and reverential love bound him
to Wagner the man. He took a personal share
in everything that distressed or delighted Wagner, and abusive attacks upon the Master and
his family aroused his indignation as keenly as
if they had been directed against himself. It
was for him an absolute and heartfelt necessity
to share the work which piled up about Wagner,
and to help remove the obstacles which threatened to bar his pathway towards the goal."

Emil Heckel of Mannheim was the founder
of the first Wagner Society, and was ever an
active outside agitator and organiser. To him
was intrusted the chief part of the business
connected with the organising and developing of
a Society of Patrons, by which it was hoped
that the great undertaking could be effectively
financed.

Carl Brandt was the famous stage machinist of Darmstadt, whose task went far beyond that of the specific province of scenic machinery to include everything that had to do with creating a suitable home for the art work of the future.

Wagner's appreciation of his services found frequent expression. In one of his earlier letters to Brandt he writes:

" You understand perfectly what is at stake, and this you would not be able to do did you not possess the proper imagination and genuine inventiveness."

And again:

" Without you no Nibelung, you know that!"

# BAYREUTH

## May, 1871–May, 1872

How did Wagner, in the pursuit of his plans for the realisation of his Festival Idea, happen to decide upon the quiet old Bavarian town of Bayreuth?

The answer to this question he gives in a letter to Friedrich Feustel:

" The place must not be a large city with a permanent theatre, nor one of the larger summer resorts, where during the season an absolutely undesirable public would offer itself; it must be centrally located in Germany, and moreover be a Bavarian city, as I also intend to take up my permanent residence in the place, and consider that I could do this only in Bavaria, if I hope to enjoy the continued patronage of the King of Bavaria. Apart from these considerations, this pleasant old city, with its surroundings, made an indelible impression upon me years ago, and the fact that I am an utter stranger to the citizens of Bayreuth gives me no cause for alarm."

In the spring of 1871 he revisited the city unofficially, to confirm the "indelible impressions" of his early youth, and again fell under the charm of the quaint old town nestling among the hills of central Germany and surrounded by the nimbus of a not uninteresting history.

It was during this *incognito* visit that Wagner suddenly fell ill, and the leading physician of the place was called in by the host of the inn "Die Sonne" to see a patient by the name of Richard Wagner. After performing his professional duties the physician entered into a conversation with his patient, during the course of which the identity of the latter was revealed.

"Who could have dreamed of such a thing and foretold to me yesterday that to-day I was to make the acquaintance of the world-famous master!"

Out of this casual acquaintance, the very first which Wagner had made in Bayreuth, grew a warm personal friendship, and Dr. Carl Landgraf became not only the family physician but the faithful house friend, in whose charge the little family was always left when Wagner and his wife were away on the repeated tours which were to give an impetus to the Bayreuth fund.

In addition to his professional duties at Wahnfried, this altruistic man was the unofficial but uncompensated physician of the artistic *personnel* of the Festival, and therefore it is quite fitting that the first letter of the " Bayreuth " collection should be addressed to Dr. Carl Landgraf.

### To Dr. Carl Landgraf

(Leipzig, May 11, 1871.)

*Most esteemed Sir!*

I am not coming back to Bayreuth this time, as I promised you, and you will not see me again until late in the summer. I make this announcement, because I should not like you to consider me ungrateful. I herewith acknowledge myself as your debtor; your draught did me excellent service.

As for the rest, it is now decided that my great Stage Festival Play shall take place in the summer of 1873 in Bayreuth, at which time I also intend to take up my permanent residence in your city. In order that you, of whose friendly good-will I am thoroughly convinced, may be in a position to contradict all false reports as to my enterprise, I take pleasure in informing you that while it is true that His Majesty, the King of Bavaria, has granted his permission for such an undertaking, and will give considerable financial support to the same, it will nevertheless remain my personal affair, and can only be carried to a successful issue by a far-reaching coalition of the friends of my art. Consequently, just as any other person who starts out on an enterprise, I shall have to create friendly relations with the city authorities of Bayreuth; but I believe I am justified in counting upon their ready co-operation, when the significance and prominence into which the city will thereby be brought is taken into consideration.

Late in the summer I shall arrange a meeting in Bayreuth, with the necessary competent persons, in order to choose and purchase the site upon which to erect my Festival Theatre, work upon which is to be commenced immediately. At the same time I shall decide upon a building site for my own residence, and I should be greatly obliged to you if at your leisure you could assist me in finding something desirable. I had already discussed a pretty piece of meadow-land bordering on the castle park with the steward of the castle; this lot, however, is entirely lacking in a few old trees. I should be pleased if you could find out something about this for me! In the hope of being able to greet you personally in a few months, I remain, with the greatest esteem,

Yours most faithfully,

RICHARD WAGNER.

(Lucerne. Triebschen.)

## To Emil Heckel

(Lucerne, May 19, 1871.)

*Honoured Sir!*

Deeply grateful for the kindnesses you have shown me, I welcome, first of all, your decision, which I have just learned, of taking an active part in the realisation of our great undertaking. I recognise fully the value of your decision, and beg you to apply to Herr K(arl) Tausig, 35, Dessauer str : Berlin, for further information in the matter.

He has assumed the temporary management until a Committee of Patrons can be organised, and will give you exact information as to the manner in which your participation can be made most effective.

With the kindest greetings,

Yours sincerely,

RICHARD WAGNER.

In April, 1871, Wagner had sent out communication and appeal to the friends of his art

" About the Performance of his Stage Festival Play, ' Ring of the Nibelung,' " in which the thoughts contained in the preface to the text of the drama were once more emphasised.

The first thing was to organise a society of friends and patrons of the great undertaking, and Karl Tausig (Berlin), Emil Heckel (Mannheim), and Baroness Marie von Schleinitz (now Countess von Wolkenstein) assumed the task of drawing up a plan for a Society of Patrons, and of making the effort to secure the necessary number of subscribers.

The entire cost of the Festival was estimated at three hundred thousand thalers (about $225,000) — a sum which was to be raised by disposing of one thousand certificates of membership at three hundred thalers each. The holder of such a certificate was entitled to a place for all the performances, and it was also possible for three persons to participate in one of these certificates.

Karl Tausig, who was the life and soul of the

project, and who also cherished the idea of organising an orchestra to give special concerts for the cause, and later to form the nucleus of the Festival orchestra, died at the early age of thirty.

The burden of the work then fell upon Emil Heckel, who also conceived the idea of calling into existence the Wagner Societies, by which persons of unlimited means would be given an opportunity of taking part in the work.

The first Wagner Society was organised in Mannheim in 1871, the members paying annual dues of five florins, in return for which they received a numbered ticket. Thirty-five of these tickets bought a Patron's Certificate, the possession of which was decided by lot, and the remaining thirty-four holders of tickets had to console themselves with the consciousness of having contributed to a worthy cause.

Similar societies were organised in Vienna, Munich, and Leipzig, and by April, 1874, twenty-five cities had leagued themselves together to make possible the Bayreuth enterprise. Not only German but foreign cities rallied to Wagner's support; among them, London, Petersburgh, Brussels, and New York.[1]

## To Carl Brandt

(Lucerne, August 20, 1871.)

*My dear Co-worker!*

At this moment I have no more direct cause for writing you than the one arising out of the very pleasant remembrance of our last meeting.

I feel impelled to repeat more clearly upon paper what I said to you verbally when we parted. It is truly a great joy for me to have found you! A great share of the success of my undertaking is now assured by your co-operation. I was genuinely encouraged to find you so closely acquainted with my intentions. You understand perfectly what is at stake, and this you would not be able to do did you not possess the necessary imagination and genuine inventiveness re-

[1] From Henry T. Finck's "Wagner and his Works," Vol. II.

quired here. Certain directions which you specified to the architect really surprised me; the ex-
tension of the proscenium was an inspiration on
your part, which crowns the entire idea of the
interior of the theatre.

As I thought over all this again to-day, it
became an absolute necessity to express to you
the great confidence you have inspired, as well
as my genuine joy at having found you. May
you receive this in an equally friendly spirit!

Within the next few days I expect definite
news as to the outside participation in my
undertaking.

In the meantime I have received deputies from
the "Wagner Societies," who have reported
quite encouraging news. Without doubt everything will work out all right, and you also, esteemed friend, will find your reward in a proper
appreciation.

With cordial greetings,

Yours sincerely,

RICHARD WAGNER.

## To Emil Heckel

*Honoured Sir!*

Pardon the delay in my answer! I have been occupied of late in a lively correspondence in regard to the most immediate steps necessary for the commencement of my undertaking. This will suffer a decided backset if we are not able to begin the preliminary work on the building of the theatre this autumn. It is very important to ascertain the present amount of the contributions, and to decide accordingly as to whether the necessary contracts can be given to the architects and machinists; if the time which I have set is to be kept, the preliminary work must be begun at once. . . .

When the circumstances are favourable, I intend to meet the architect and the machinist in Bayreuth the end of October, to determine everything necessary for the laying of the corner-stone, to which event I intend to invite you, esteemed sir, as well as the committees of the other societies. In every respect such a meeting (in connection with which I should address a word to the general public) would be advantageous for the progress of the undertaking, and for this reason I wish very keenly to carry out my plans, even if later delays unavoidably occur. . . .

With the warmest recognition of your kind services to me, and with the request that you present my compliments to our valued friends in Mannheim, I remain

Yours respectfully,

RICHARD WAGNER.


## To FRIEDRICH FEUSTEL

(LUCERNE, November 1, 1871.)

*Honoured Sir!*

Through my dear nephew, Clement Brockhaus of Leipzig, the delightful assurance has reached me that you would meet me half-way if I approached you in the not unimportant matter which has already been brought to your notice.

As to the undertaking itself, I take the liberty of sending you under separate cover a more detailed explanation of the same. My reasons for choosing Bayreuth as the place of the execution of my plans will not be difficult to divine (even without the further particulars which I shall reserve for some future time) from the demands which I have made upon the place. . . . [Here follows paragraph already quoted on page 17.]

With this preface, permit me to make you more familiar with my affairs.

In the first place, there are various not unimportant points upon which I should like information.

I take it for granted that the city of Bayreuth is in no way to be called upon in collecting the funds for my undertaking. Energetic friends of my cause are already employed in collecting the necessary sums, and I already feel myself justified, by their success, in taking the necessary steps to secure a site for the erection of my provisionary theatre, the commencement of which, on account of the unfavourableness of the season, must be postponed until next March.

I should esteem myself particularly fortunate if, by your kind permission, I could turn to you, highly honoured sir, in the settlement of these important preliminary questions. The first of these is the choice and acquisition of a building site. The chief thing to me seems to be whether the city of Bayreuth, in consideration of the advantages accruing to the city from my undertaking (both as regards her reputation as well as the increased intercourse with strangers), is in a position to promise, or feels herself moved to offer me, free of charge, a piece of ground for the erection of my theatre. I will not say that my undertaking is absolutely dependent upon such support; but it must be clear to anyone that such concessions will tend to establish from the very outset pleasant relations between the city of Bayreuth and my undertaking. In the event that such willingness is shown, there can be no question of a choice of place on my part. . . .

I have further to mention the chief objection which has been made against Bayreuth on the part of my patrons, and that is their anxiety that sufficient accommodation for the guests cannot be found. It will be necessary to insure satisfactory entertainment to a *personnel* of two hundred persons — in the height of the season.

As my experience furnishes me with no suggestion, I leave this point with you for your kind consideration, and should be very much pleased if you could put me in possession of information which would serve to quiet the anxieties of my patrons. It would also be a comfort to me to feel assured that there would be no lack of workmen for the rapid erection of the building, and that we should not find ourselves crippled by a strike. . . .

I add at once to my report the settlement of another point, namely, that it will devolve upon me, as was signified to me in Munich, to secure the approval of the city authorities for my entire undertaking.

It would be well to keep in mind the fact that this has nothing to do with a money-making theatrical enterprise; the performances will be attended only by invited guests and the patrons of the undertaking; no one will be allowed to pay for admission. On the other hand, I have already provided for a sufficient number of seats to be placed at the disposal of the citizens of Bayreuth — these to be distributed free of charge.

Having, I believe, informed you, highly honoured sir, of the chief points, which I felt encouraged to submit for your kind consideration, advice, and co-operation, permit me to beg the favour of a favourable answer, as well as to assure you of the great esteem with which I have the honour to salute you as

Yours most faithfully,

RICHARD WAGNER.

## To Emil Heckel

(Lucerne, November 9, 1871.)

*Most esteemed Herr Heckel!*

Your suggestion is a most excellent one; if such an alliance could be formed, it would be exactly what I could wish. Just now the strength of the situation lies in the strong individual organisations. It is the individual society which offers at present the most effective support. The Society "Wagneriana" in Berlin recently decided to take sixty Patron's Certificates and guarantees the entire orchestra. Vienna *promises*, at least, to prove herself most generous during the course of the winter.

In Leipzig, on the other hand, only three-fourths of a Patrons' Certificate has been reported; in Munich — through the Society — nothing has been accomplished, as far as I know.

It is only in Mannheim that you have proven yourselves active. None the less I realise that only by means of a big universal alliance can the undertaking be assured in a permanent and successful sense, and therefore I consider your suggestions as particularly worthy of notice. . . .

In Bayreuth everything is going ahead in the most inspiring manner; my wishes are being met with great seriousness. I shall take all the necessary steps in regard to the building site (which the city presumably will present me) in order that work may begin in March. . . .

For the present the most important thing seems to be to send out a vigorous and sharply accentuated appeal, according to the plan which you outlined for me. As a result of this, we can then see what has been accomplished by next March, and *then* an assembling of the committees in Bayreuth (for the corner-stone laying) would have especial significance.

I hope you are of my opinion, and will have the kindness to impart my ideas to Herr v. Loën, at the same time giving him my cordial greetings.

Respectfully yours,

RICHARD WAGNER.

## To Emil Heckel

(Lucerne, November 13, 1871.)

*Esteemed Sir!*

I return at once your outline, of which I quite approve. May the matter now take its course and the Germans show that they at least understand how to bestow the proper attention upon such serious and persistent efforts for an ignominiously neglected branch of public art, and yet one of such unlimited possibilities as this to which I am devoting my life. It is encouraging to meet with a man of your stamp, Herr Heckel!

A great number of copies of the green pamphlet on the performance of the " Ring of the Nibelung " are at your disposal for the purpose of distribution. If you like, I will send you some.

In regard to money matters I beg of you to keep in touch with Herr v. Loën. The banker Cohn has also agreed to see that the various sums are placed at interest until they need to be used.

With expressions of my esteem,

Yours respectfully,

RICHARD WAGNER.


To FRIEDRICH FEUSTEL

(LUCERNE, November 23, 1871.)

*Highly esteemed Sir!*

Your capital news was not necessary — however much it delighted me for utilitarian and other reasons — to strengthen me in my carefully considered intentions. I shall not attempt to deny, however, that it had something of this effect. You only confirmed the suggesting of my good spirit which brought to my memory, from my far-distant youth, the city of Bayreuth, lying almost unknown and unnoticed in the centre of Germany, when I was looking about for a spot of German soil upon which I could establish a home for myself.

Now that we have gone so far, offers from

other sources are beginning to reach me in regard to my undertaking.  The City Council of Baden-Baden offers me a building site gratis; Darmstadt also offers to build a theatre according to my plans and place it at my disposal during the summer months.  I feel convinced that I shall never regret having refused these offers. . . .

With the most cordial and respectful greetings, I remain

Yours sincerely,

RICHARD WAGNER.

## To CARL BRANDT

(LUCERNE, November 25, 1871.)

Tell me, my worthy friend and companion, what is the matter with you?  You are silent and silent, and moreover one hears nothing from Berlin about you?

In the meantime I was obliged to arrive at an understanding with Neumann, and it has now developed that the building cannot be commenced before the end of March next year; by the way, he was ready to vouch that you could be ready by that time.

In the meantime Bayreuth has done a great deal — gratuitous building site, etc. Baden also made a similar offer. The telegraph wires were congested in behalf of Darmstadt — in fact, with such marvellous things of all sorts; which I could only explain to myself by the fact that they proposed to make an arrangement with me in order to be able to rebuild their theatre which was burned down (!!) And still you remain silent!

May your silence not signify that your zeal for my undertaking has grown cold! . . . Without you no Nibelung — you must know that! Cordial greetings from

Yours faithfully,

RICHARD WAGNER.

## To Carl Brandt

*Esteemed Friend!*

In reply to your kind letter just received, I inform you briefly of the following facts. . . .

I have long since reconciled myself to the postponement of our performance until the year 1874, but I do not yet admit it. . . . The Darmstadt reports I could have explained at once, as you did later. I understand and appreciate your ideas perfectly, as well as your excellent intentions. And surely I shall soon convince you that even under the most favourable circumstances I can have nothing to do with the Darmstadt theatre. Here it is a case of either this — or that! Wholly — or not at all!

Only one thing I wish to remark: you frightened me by the news that you had left the Semper plans with the Grand Duke. Do not forget that these are the property of the King of Bavaria (dearly bought, and only intrusted to me for the purpose of my enterprise, and to which I consider myself authorised, in the name of the King of Bavaria, for use only in a Bavarian city).

As, according to repeated experience, the greatest possible unpleasantness could arise from this, I beg of you, in whatever way seems to you the most advisable, to leave the Semper plans entirely out of the question. Should the Grand Duke find them to his liking, the only thing to do would be to advise him to apply directly to Semper. The latter would then know how far he was at liberty to make use of his own property without trespassing upon the rights of the King of Bavaria. . . .

With cordial greetings,

Yours,

RICHARD WAGNER.

The plans to which Wagner here refers were those drawn up by Gottfried Semper, at that time Professor of Architecture at the Polytech-

nic Institute in Zurich. King Ludwig's plans
for helping his favourite to the realisation of
his ideas in regard to a performance of the
" Ring of the Nibelung " included the erection of a monumental Festival Theatre on the
banks of the Isar, on the site occupied by the
Maximilianeum.

At Wagner's suggestion Semper was summoned from Zurich in 1865 for a conference in
regard to the projected theatre, which was to
cost three and a half millions of guldens. But
before Semper's model arrived in Munich, feeling against Wagner had reached such a crisis
that, in order not to endanger the peace of his
land, King Ludwig was obliged to yield to the
pressure of Wagner's enemies and beg the composer to return to his Swiss exile, providing him,
however, with a full year's salary.

Frustrated in his plans for a Festival Theatre,
the order to Semper was countermanded, and all
that remains of the high-minded project of King
Ludwig is the model which stands in the Na-

tional Museum in Munich, instead of the monumental structure which was to crown the heights overlooking the city.

### To Friedrich Feustel

(Munich, December 12, 1871.)

*Esteemed Sir!*

I beg your indulgence when I inform you that I intend leaving here to-morrow evening (Wednesday) and expect to arrive in Bayreuth on the early train. To this information I add the request that you will exert all your influence in making it possible to settle all the necessary business in connection with the great enterprise to which you have pledged your active co-operation during the time between Thursday and Saturday noon. For unfortunately my time is very much occupied. Thursday I expect to receive Building Inspector Neumann of Berlin, as well as the Master Machinist Carl Brandt of Darmstadt.

The first thing to be looked after will be the

building site for the theatre, as well as the necessary decisions in regard to the same which are
to be arranged with the worthy council of the
city magistrates. The choice of a situation for
my own residence lies also very near my heart.
A conference with the Court Architect Wölffel,
and also the Berlin architect, in regard to the
contracts, and the possibility of the adjustment
of the question with which I was obliged to
trouble you in regard to the accommodations of
our future guests, will form the close of our
discussion. . . .

In agreeable anticipation of making your
valued personal acquaintance, I am

Yours respectfully,

RICHARD WAGNER.

TO CARL BRANDT

(LUCERNE, December 26, 1871.)

*My dear Friend!*

Accept my sincere thanks for your faithful-
ness in coming and amiability of endurance! It

was delightful, and I shall never forget (nor will anyone of the others) how in the depth of winter we sought out the ground for the art work of the " future." Surely it was well chosen, and we three confederates will not conduct ourselves badly on this new Grütli. . . . Now, my dear sir, I hope you have gotten rid of your " Melancolie " and think actively of our work.

Do not hesitate to give any necessary order; send me all of your contracts to be signed, and Feustel will be immediately instructed and empowered to make the corresponding payments.

For the rest, everything remains according to our recent agreement. Everything which time and circumstances will permit will be got in readiness; in May we shall meet again, and I hope by that time to have the co-operation of a few competent painters for the production of the scenic sketches.

Sympathy for my undertaking has made such significant progress that there is no longer any

doubt as to the sure and certain accomplishment
of the same.

With the most friendly greetings,

Yours faithfully,

RICHARD WAGNER.


The allusion here to the " new Grütli " refers
to a scene in Schiller's drama of " Wilhelm Tell,"
when the three confederates, Werner Stauf-
facher, Walter Fürst, and Arnold von Melchtal,
from the three Swiss cantons of Ury, Schweiz,
a..d Unterwalden, met at a lonely spot on the
banks of Lake Lucerne and bound themselves
by an oath to deliver their countrymen from the
oppression of the Austrian yoke. This impressive scene has been immortalised in a fresco on
the walls of the little Tell chapel, which attracts
its large quota of tourists each season.

Equally solemn and significant seemed to
Wagner the confederacy into which he had entered with his associates, Neumann the Berlin
architect and Carl Brandt the stage machinist,

for the realisation of a plan which was to emancipate German art.


## To Muncker and Feustel

(Lucerne, December 26, 1871.)

*My esteemed Sirs!*

The decision of the two Councils of the city
of Bayreuth — by the terms of which the ground
necessary for the building of a Festival Theatre,
together with the roads and grounds belonging
thereto, on the chosen location in the vicinity
of St. George, are placed at my disposal free of
charge — contains for me a cause for especial
gratitude, which I beg of you to express most
cordially, in my name, to the highly esteemed
gentlemen of both Councils.

Although my most sanguine expectations led
me to hope for nothing more than a friendly
reception, which would enable me to choose Bayreuth as the long-sought location for my Festival performance, I now confess with great satisfaction, that my joy at the fulfilment of my

wishes has been increased in great measure by the hospitable attitude expressed by this decision.

During the successful progress of my undertaking I hope it will be possible to convince you what significance I permit myself to attach to the fact that my idea in regard to a remodelling of the German art organism is to be concentrated for its realisation in a definite local scheme, which local scheme will serve as a model for performances elsewhere.

That to the considerations which influence me in my choice of Bayreuth is now to be added the very encouraging and hospitable advances of the magistrates of this city, gives me the most confident security in the ultimate realisation of my hopes and wishes.

Again begging you, most esteemed sirs, to convey the cordial expression of my gratitude to the members of both Councils of the city of Bayreuth, and with the hope of seeing you soon again, I am

Yours very faithfully,

RICHARD WAGNER.

On December 15, 1871, the city magistrates formally placed at Wagner's disposal a piece of ground in the Stückberg for his Festival Theatre, and promised in addition that several acres of ground should be laid out as a park. But at the last moment one of the owners of this piece of property withdrew his consent, and the City Council had to look about for a new location.

This they found on the heights to the south of the city, where the present provisionary theatre now stands, the enforced exchange proving eventually to be more advantageous.

### To Friedrich Feustel

(Lucerne, December 31, 1871.
New Year's Eve.)

*Esteemed Sir and valued Friend!*

With deep emotion I received your card to-day. At the time I sent off my — in a certain measure — official document, I had already determined to employ the first leisure hour in recalling myself again personally to your memory.

As I have recognized from the first, esteemed friend, you are, of a truth, of particular significance in my future, in fact in my life plans.

I need a friend of your stamp.

Your great simplicity at once allowed me a glimpse into the energetic traits of your character. I can fully rely not only on your openheartedness but also on your keen intelligence.

With this in mind, I shall retain in the future your proffered hand. . . .

Since our great cause has now taken such a favourable turn, I have but little more to tell you in regard to it. The most important thing is that I have taken the necessary measures by which the payment of the present contracts will be made possible by the conveyance of the funds now held by Herr v. Loën. I am further considering how the entire management of the business can best be transferred to Bayreuth after the first of May.

Here my energetic co-operation must be counted upon, as otherwise a central point would be hard to find, and therefore my consent hitherto withheld in calm expectation (of this time) has recently been given.

I expect therefore that an executive committee will be formed here in Bayreuth, which will be empowered by the delegates from the Society of Patrons — at the time of the corner-stone laying in May — to assume control of the entire enterprise.

For this reason I regard it as necessary that I should not be away from Bayreuth for any length of time, and should now take up my permanent residence there.

Your friendly aid is indispensable in regard to this important point.

You know that I shall not be able to take possession of my house until the autumn of 1873. What shall I do in order that I and my family shall not be too seriously incommoded during this interval? This is the question in the solution of which I turn to you. It will certainly be difficult to find suitable accommodation in the city of Bayreuth itself, and it would be impossible for me to confine my numerous little family in a small house with a restricted city garden after the wide and delightful freedom which they have enjoyed here.

I have in mind one of those large earlier estates of the nobility, pointed out to me as "castles," with large gardens, in fact, "parks," one or two hours distant from the city, which were offered me as a permanent residence. As such I immediately refused them — as *permanent* I mean — because I wished to settle in the immediate vicinity of the city. . . .

The point now is to secure something desirable and rent it for a year and a half. I shall have to learn to adapt myself to the distance during this time, and shall have to make some arrangement about a horse and carriage until I am permanently settled.

As you were kind enough to promise me your friendly aid in regard to my personal needs also, I, first of all, beg your assistance in this point.

How it would delight me if you could hold out an encouraging prospect to me! I should set about looking for a temporary residence in Dresden with great reluctance, but, on the other hand, should nothing offer itself in Bayreuth, I should be obliged to do so, as I must leave my present asylum (although I have possession of it until October, 1873) in order to be as near the centre of Germany next spring as is made imperative by the importance of my affairs.

You certainly understand this perfectly, and I have nothing to repeat, as I am filled with the greatest confidence in you, and with this feeling beg you to accept the most cordial greetings from me and my dear wife and also to remember us kindly to your dear ones.

With true esteem,

Yours most faithfully,

RICHARD WAGNER.

At this time Wagner was still living at Villa Triebschen near Lucerne, a spot which had

proven a " blessed asylum " for him when political animosity had forced him to leave Munich
and his royal benefactor.

This Triebschen period is full of significance,
as it was here that " Die Meistersinger " was
written, and the music drama of " Siegfried "
was completed after a decade and a half of
disheartening interruption.

It was during the Triebschen days that the
obstacles were removed which made it possible
for Wagner to unite himself with Cosima von
Bülow, the daughter of Franz Liszt and the
Countess D'Agoult, and the wife of Hans von
Bülow at the time that she came into Wagner's
life.

Here Siegfried Wagner was born, and it was
this long-wished event, the birth of a son, which
gave to the musical world the beautiful Siegfried Idyll.

Under Wagner's direction the work was performed by a little company of musicians and
friends on the steps of the Triebschen Villa, and

Frau Wagner was overcome by the unexpected serenade.

Thus there is a close link connecting Trieb-schen and Bayreuth, and it is not too much to say that the calm and quiet of the Triebschen period gave the direct impulse to the Bayreuth Idea.

### To Emil Heckel

(Lucerne, January 3, 1872.)

*To the Five Just Men, Salutations and Blessings!*[1]

Allow me to thank you, my esteemed friend, for your faithful zeal! . . .

I should like to learn something of the general condition of our affairs. I am building away here in Bayreuth without knowing but that in the end we shall be left in the lurch. In May all of you must make up your minds to establish the general treasury in Bayreuth, with my excel-lent friend, the banker Feustel. I now see that

---

[1] This was the playful way in which Wagner characterised the five men who composed the Executive Committee of the Mannheim Wagner Society: Emil Heckel, Dr. Zeroni, Ferdinand Lange, Hänlein, and Koch.

I must begin to have a word to say, in order to give the undertaking a focussing point.

I believe the " just men " will support me! . . . As for the rest, I place all sorts of pleasant anticipation in the German national spirit, upon which I am so dependent! . . .

That which gives me pleasure is a man of your sort, valued friend; you know what — and why?

A thousand thanks for all the friendly tokens of your kindness and love; I have taken cognisance of them with great emotion!

Again cordial greetings from

Yours faithfully,

RICHARD WAGNER.

(Former favourite of the European Court.)


To FRIEDRICH FEUSTEL

(LUCERNE, February 7, 1872.)

*My esteemed dear Friend!*

You are the last person to whom I am writing since my return; for two days I have done nothing but write letters, and have only got round to you late in the evening; so it is with friendship! The friend comes last, because we know with certainty that it is he alone who has patience and forbearance.

We expect in a few days a report as to the success of the Vienna Society, that the favourable news may be used in lending interest to the corner-stone laying — an interest which I intend to increase by an extraordinary musical performance for which I have already taken the preparatory steps.

Under all circumstances my goal remains the same, and the certainty of reaching it is guaranteed by my move to Bayreuth. . . . That, however, which fills me deeply with courage and composure is the fact that I have gained *you*, my friend! Had I not encountered you on my way to the goal — you, and the characteristics and intellectual traits which you possess — I should possibly have recoiled before the difficulties, and relinquished the idea of absolving my task. And yet there is one thing which stands above all others, and that is the depth of my artistic conviction as it manifests itself in the consciousness of my mission. That now, on the rough pathway mapped out for me by this mission, I find *you*, my friend, — and moreover, *as* you are, *who* you are, and *where* you are, — I recognise as the fulfilment of a profound decree of fate, and you will have to accept the position and consent to be regarded by me as "endæmonic"! . . . Some patience will be necessary, but above all things you must have faith and courage. We must wait and see what the next few weeks bring. . . .

In the meantime the entire Triebschen sends greetings to the dear Feustel house in Bayreuth! . . .

Farewell, dear friend! I am happy when I even think of you. Greetings to all friends, above all, your dear ones, and be assured of my genuine gratitude for your friendship.

Yours,

RICHARD WAGNER.

### To Burgomaster Theodor Muncker

(Lucerne, February 10, 1872.)

*Dear and valued Friend!*

As you were kind enough to assume the temporary planting of my newly acquired building lot, and as there is no more time to be lost, I take the liberty of availing myself of your kindness, and disclosing to you my most casual plans in regard to the same.

I have indicated the desired position of my house on the accompanying photograph, and also a rough sketch of the division of the lot. A road will lead from the street to the court, which would best be an *allée* of chestnut trees. On either side of the *allée* are to be fruit and vegetable gardens, shut off by a hedge, the outer boundaries, however, to be planted with shrubbery and groups of pine trees in the corners.

Between the house and the castle park we shall lay out the real decorative garden. First of all, there will be a big round lawn in the middle which later can be intersected by flower-beds; in this space noble trees, such as plantains, catalfa, etc., must be properly distributed. Here, again, the side toward the castle park demands much close shrubbery, with trees of various species and, in the corners, pine and fir trees.

On account of the season the most important thing is to see that a goodly number of trees and shrubs are planted in the manner indicated, and that too much, rather than too little, shall be expended upon it.

A clever gardener, whom you, dear friend, would choose for me, could possibly work out a tentative plan for the laying out of the entire piece of ground according to the appended approximate specifications; I should then be able from here to indicate my wishes more exactly, and in this way a beginning would have been made.

I feel sure that this cannot be entrusted to anyone more competent than yourself, in conjunction with our excellent friend Feustel. I expect the definite plans for my house any day;

according to all promises made to me, they must soon be here, and even before the end of the month everything for further settlement shall be in your hands.

May God grant that our great undertaking may also soon come into an encouraging channel; I am of good courage, because I know that for the greater part it rests in the hands of my Bayreuth friends! My dear wife and I think with great satisfaction on the fact that we shall soon belong entirely to you; remain kindly disposed toward me!

With the most cordial greetings — also to our dear friend Feustel — I remain,

Your grateful and faithful,

RICHARD WAGNER.

To EMIL HECKEL

(LUCERNE, February 16, 1872.)

*Dear just Man!*

Please accept my belated thanks for your Bayreuth visit as well as your report of your recent

Berlin adventure! And in order to come at once to the gravest point in connection with the latter, I beg of you to say that under no circumstances will I give my consent to this projected lottery.

There can really be nothing more humiliating than the position into which I have been forced by exaggerated reports as to the significance of a "Wagneriana" in Berlin, and by being thus made to believe that I could accept such assistance which, of a certainty, would drive me on to the shoals.

If anyone should offer me two hundred thousand thalers toward the realisation of my idea, I should be profoundly grateful to such a person; on the other hand, to ask of me the authorisation for a lottery seems to be simply a swindle which cannot be too firmly repulsed. . . .

It seems also premature to me, valued friend, to issue a proclamation in regard to a society the aim of which is placed far beyond the goal which lies nearest and yet is so difficult to reach, namely, the first performance of my Festival Play. Every possible effort will be necessary to ensure the attainment of this goal; I shall accomplish it if I am patiently supported; my chief anxiety on this point is directed towards my dependence upon the King of Bavaria.

I am already recruiting for the Ninth Symphony, and expect definite news soon in regard to the instrumentalists.

If the laying of the corner-stone goes off according to my programme, I hope for much assistance from the impression it makes.

Cordial greetings for your colleagues, the just men. Hoping to see you soon in Bayreuth!

Yours most devotedly,

RICHARD WAGNER.

## To FRIEDRICH FEUSTEL

(LUCERNE, February 25, 1872.)

*My dear Friend!*

I cannot tell you how sorry I am to be obliged to turn over my business to you in such a confused condition! But nothing would be gained by giving way to such feelings. Upon closer inspection there is only a bad stage to be passed through into which we have temporarily been thrown by neglect in a matter in itself full of hope and promise. If things take a good course, we shall have only good results from this previous neglect, that is, if they are now managed cleverly and wisely! This is my consolation and encouragement!

The chief thing now is the favourable outcome of my project for May 22. I did not wish to make anything public until I had secured the consent of my musicians and singers. According to the latest information which has reached me the success of the undertaking is beyond all doubt. Everywhere my invitation has been received with enthusiasm, and the acceptance of the best musicians of the leading German orchestras reach me in almost overwhelming numbers. And no less on the part of the singers. Therefore I can now give you authority to enter into an agreement for the work on the orchestra pit. . . . I am to receive the plans for my house this week. In the meantime I thank you heartily for your trouble about the garden plot. Yes, my Bayreuth friends, that is the right stamp! I had indeed a prophetic feeling!

I look on quietly and modestly at your arrangements concerning the commencement of work on the theatre. Without doubt the chief thing is to save the situation by putting as bold a face on the matter as possible.

For the rest, I breathe freely at the thought of not seeing the enormous undertaking hurried through with, particularly from an artistic standpoint. . . .

Our children are already romancing about Bayreuth; it is difficult for us to endure it here so long, so far from our new friends.

My blessings upon you and sincerest greetings!

Yours,

RICHARD WAGNER.

The ceremonies in connection with the cornerstone laying of the new theatre were to close with a Festival Concert, of which the outstanding feature was to be Beethoven's Ninth Symphony.

It was to take place in the old Margravian Theatre, the orchestral pit of which had to be enlarged to accommodate the large number of musicians who had volunteered their services for this great musical event.

To Burgomaster Theodor Muncker

(Lucerne, March 26, 1872.)

*My excellent Friend!*

. . . I must address myself especially to you, in order to prepare you for the anxieties which you will necessarily encounter so long as you remain favourably disposed toward my great undertaking, as it has now become our mutual care.

So many obstacles have arisen that I consider it all the more important that we hold to our Preliminary Festival on May 22, which, assuming the issue to be for certain a favourable one, will bring with it a more vigorous impulse to our great undertaking.

My invitation, which was presented to you for signature, will have informed you that everything is already in the most flourishing condition. In fact, my appeal has been met far beyond my expectations, for we have to provide for four hundred instead of three hundred musical guests.

In addition to the increased demands upon Bayreuth hospitality, the following difficulty in regard to our further arrangements grows out of this interest. The space in our opera house will need to contain one hundred more singers and proportionately one hundred more hosts. . . .

We must see how many acceptances come in from our patrons and friends as the result of our invitation; as only *one symphony* is to be performed this time, I shall quite understand if these notifications do not prove to be many. Presumably, therefore, the auditorium will prove adequate, in spite of the fact that we are to place four hundred free seats at the disposal of our Bayreuth hosts.

But now comes a bad piece of business, dear friend, in which I must be able to count on your friendly assistance. I shall have to leave entirely to you the appeal to the Bayreuth citizens who are willing to offer hospitality to the musicians and singers for three days, although I naturally place my name entirely at your disposal and pleasure.

I intend to instruct all of my scattered musicians and singers to send in their names and addresses to you personally. . . . We will have four hundred invitation forms printed, to which will be added the address of the respective Bayreuth hosts. These invitation forms will then be sent to the various organizations or (in certain cases) to the individual guests in due time, so that each guest will know who his entertainer is to be when he arrives in Bayreuth. More definite instruction for this you will receive from me in good time.

Finally, I confess to you, my dear friend, that my present residence is becoming more and more a distressing matter to me, particularly as I see how necessary it is that I should not be so far from the centre of Germany.

The interruptions which I regret are often the result of dilatoriness, against which I shall be obliged to take energetic measures. My Berlin friend, the architect Neumann, gives me very little comfort; everything is dragging vexatiously; his plans and drawings for my house have turned out beautifully, but what a time elapses before they are handed over to my Bayreuth friends and agents for execution! This must be done at once. Then — *your* troubles begin again!

But you do it gladly; I have noticed this, dear friend, with pleasure. So I remain of good courage, and send you greetings from a grateful heart.

Your deeply devoted

RICHARD WAGNER.

## To Feustel and Muncker

(Lucerne, April 7, 1872.)

*To my dear and highly esteemed Friends, Messrs.
Feustel and Muncker!*

You must permit me to write to you mutually,
for you are, as I know, *one* heart and *one* soul
in my cause, and it would therefore be difficult
to decide what, of all I have to impart, should
be said to either one separately!

Moreover, it is unnecessary to impress upon
you to what a great degree your kind letter re-
freshed and strengthened me.

For a long time I have cherished the wish —
greater even than for the success of my artistic
activity — to have a quiet home, in which I
should be able to strengthen my overtaxed mental powers by getting out of harness; and I
have wished this all the more of late years, since
the noble blessing of an incomparably happy
family life has been granted me.

This wish, more than anything else, influenced

me in my choice of your dear city of Bayreuth, and since I have known you, my dear friends, and through you gained an insight into the friendly attitude of your city toward me, the consideration of settling in your midst has really outweighed the success of my unusual artistic undertaking.

This I have given the King of Bavaria to understand unconditionally; and this I had a right to do, as one of the first assurances which I received from him was in connection with this one point, that I was to be raised above all the cares of life and be allowed to pursue uninterruptedly my artistic activity. . . .

Although I have learned that the King has finally become reconciled to the state of things, I still deem it advisable to renounce his help in my proposed move to Bayreuth, if I cling firmly to my plans and wishes.

I have so expressed myself recently to the Court Councillor Düfflipp, and shall remain firm in refusing the support of the King in my removal to Bayreuth, as a result of which you, dear Herr Feustel, will be requested eventually to dispose of the building lot which was bought at the expense of the Royal Treasury.

I confess that I almost felt myself moved, by this failure of my most ardent wish, to renounce definitely all my plans concerning Bayreuth. But your two splendid letters have thoroughly changed my views. Let us, then, remain firm! The *work* must flourish, even should its creator be left to his former anxiety! Even without a building lot, you will probably accept me as one of your citizens. . . . We were moved to tears to learn of the care which you, dear Herr Muncker, had bestowed upon the planting and laying out of the lot intended for me. Accept my thanks, as if it were really for me!

From your intimations, dear Herr Feustel, am I to recognise that your efforts in regard to our great undertaking are being crowned with encouraging success? May I not be deceiving myself? You will encounter much indolence and unreliability, but presumably it will be the same with you as with me, namely, you will not relinquish your faith that finally — *finally* it *must* and *will* come to something with us good Germans!

Neumann is terrible! Yesterday, after receiving your letter, I telegraphed him categorically, and hope that it may have some effect. He is just a thoughtless *Berliner!* Of quite another sort is Brandt of Darmstadt! He has, in fact, the most thorough understanding of the entire matter, and how much I wish that we had also left the choice of an architect to him! Possibly we shall be obliged to call upon him, after all. Have the kindness to telegraph me immediately as to how N. has conducted himself, in order that we may accordingly adopt other measures. I fear that he has engrossed himself with plans for " my " house, which I should deplore very much, as the work, for a long time at least, has become unnecessary! In this connection I am reminded of my former plans, and in regard to them must beg of you to cancel my agreement with the host of the inn at the " Fantaisie," for which there is probably still plenty of time. My immediate move would have had for an object my proximity, when necessary, to my permanent home (now given up), as well as having furnished me with a closer point of contact for my labours in connection with the future Festival Play. As regards the latter, we are now agreed that we cannot be ready by next year, and accordingly dare not hold out a prospect of such a thing before 1874. On this point I intend to come to an understanding with my patrons on May 22 in Bayreuth.

I have now, as a simple private citizen, to take into consideration my peculiar circumstances, and find that a summer residence in the " Fantaisie " would tax me too heavily, as I still have to pay very high rent here for a year. However, I am willing to modify my decision as soon as you, my dear friend, consider my further absence from Bayreuth as injurious to our undertaking.

In regard to our Festival performance of the big Beethoven Symphony, I have hit upon a very simple expedient for the placing of my big body of singers, namely, all the singers, for whom room cannot be found on the stage, will be placed in the front rows of the parquet. In fact, this idea corresponds exactly and in the most perfect manner to my most ideal demands, according to which the public (just as the congregation in the church) shall join in the singing.

The question to be considered is that of providing for the "entertainers," in whose interests I should therefore like to suggest that all those who would prefer compensation in money rather than by a temporary art pleasure should be paid off in this way.

On the whole, I should like to have the entire parquet and stage reserved for us crazy musicians and singers, and relegate the listeners to the boxes and the balconies.

The question is now how many acceptances will come in from the patrons and friends. For that reason I regret the misunderstanding which led you to believe that I did not wish the invitation to be made public until April 15. I should like the announcement to be made at once! So much sooner we shall be clear as to whether many or, as may be easily imagined, only a moderate number of acceptances will be received.

More soon in regard to everything else! For to-day only the most friendly greetings from the depths of my soul and that of my dear wife, to you and yours!

Yours most faithfully,

RICHARD WAGNER.

The King had still secretly cherished the hope that a way would be opened by which he could recall his favourite to Munich. But intriguers were busy sowing seeds of doubt in order to create a breach between the two friends, and even though Wagner felt that the King would eventually be reconciled to the course of events, a natural feeling of pride prevented him from accepting aid from his royal friend in building a house and establishing his own *ménage* in Bayreuth. It was this feeling which led him to refuse the proffered gift of a building site.

## To FRIEDRICH FEUSTEL

(LUCERNE, April 10, 1872.)

*My dear Friend!*

Only two words in answer to your kind lines received this morning. . . . Now to serious matters!

I have no further news from Brandt. Of his *competency* I have not the slightest doubt; I should like to see him as the real director of the *artistic* management of the building also, for *he* it is who, apart from myself, possesses a real understanding of the matter. I am very anxious to see now if he will answer my invitation and put in his appearance. His demands are high, and yet I know enough to judge that he has the strange, difficult, and complicated task. If, at my first estimate, I calculated the provisionary building at a hundred thousand thalers, I allowed him also another hundred thousand for machinery and *decorations*. We can, in any case, abide by his estimates, as the decorations, as such, are calculated unnecessarily high at fifty thousand thalers.

If I reserve now the third one hundred thousand for orchestra and singers — which eventually will *not* cost so much — I shall still have a reserve fund for deficits in the building or other parts of the work. It is important now that we limit the *building* in order that here, at least approximately, we keep within the one hundred thousand thalers; this can be done less by limiting the *dimensions*, than by reducing any *unnecessary* solidity, as it is, after all, only planned to be a provisionary structure.

These are my views which I offer for friendly consideration at the renewed deliberations on this subject, which will undoubtedly be caused by the arrival of Brandt. . . .

Cordial greetings from myself and my wife, who entertains the greatest respect for you.

Yours faithfully,

RICHARD WAGNER.

## To FEUSTEL AND MUNCKER

(LUCERNE, April, 1872.)

*Highly honoured Sirs and Friends!*

With many thanks I return to you the three plans made by Herr Franck. As in the meantime I have already informed you of my wishes in regard to the placing of my musicians and singers, you may now regard the matter as settled. I however insist that *nothing* shall be changed in the first plan, upon which Herr Franck and I agreed in Bayreuth, as I regard it as entirely appropriate to the character of the performance that a part of the singers should be placed in the stalls. I have quite made up my mind as to the manner in which this is to be done, and the slightest change in the disposition of the parquet must not be attempted. I beg of you now to give me an exact statement of the number of seats in the entire parquet; at the same time it is desirable that Herr Franck should send me a plan of the interior of the theatre, in fact, a statement of the number of seats in the various parts of the building. I think that I shall need the entire parquet space, with all of its seats, for my singers, as I now have over three hundred at my disposal, and no one of whom I should like to reject — for almost moral reasons.

The real listening public would accordingly be placed almost exclusively in the galleries and rows of boxes. As the theatre is said to seat seven hundred, I count on placing two hundred in the parquet, in which number standing-room must probably also be included. According to this, we would have at our disposal only five hundred good seats for the audience. As I have to provide for four hundred (Bayreuth) hosts of our musical guests, only one hundred places would remain for patrons and friends from a distance. This number will depend upon the result of the announcement, and for that reason I should have wished that the public invitation had not been withheld so long. As it is to be no theatrical performance, I fancy, on the whole, that there will be no musical rush at that time on the part of the real "patrons," as there are not so many of them, and among them are many who (like the Emperor, twenty-five times a patron) would not dream of making the trip to Bayreuth simply to participate in this Festival.

In regard to the numbers of the Wagner Society, one could be a little careful about granting admissions. At all events, if a considerable number of really justifiable guests announced their intention of being present, then I must appeal to my Bayreuth hosts, or friends, and beg them to resign their claim of being present at the performances. Naturally there are many among them who are not very keen about a

Beethoven Symphony.  Such, then, could receive compensation from us for the proffered accommodations and meals, and it might be possible from the beginning to make two lists of entertainers, one of which would be put down as voluntary (with tickets), the other those who would be willing to accept compensation (without tickets).

At any rate, there would be a considerable amount of standing-room in the parquet (which I should not dare offer the singers), and this could be used and not be found too fatiguing for mere listeners, as the performance lasts only a little over an hour.  The chief thing is an inspiring *Musical* Festival; the chorus of the symphony should really be sung by the entire audience; in fact, it would be inspiring did they only seem to be doing so.  Therefore! be quick with the announcement, in order that we may set a limit for acceptance to be sent in; *then* a plan of the theatre and information as to the space. . . .

Levy *no duty* upon the musicians! If a musician is to take pleasure in playing well, the first condition is that he must be untrammelled. By the way, I have now exactly one hundred musicians. Accept my most cordial greetings. More later from your

Very faithful

RICHARD WAGNER.

TO FRIEDRICH FEUSTEL

(LUCERNE, April, 12 1872.)

*My esteemed Friend!*

Many thanks for your last letter! It does not occur to me to doubt the genuine success of our great undertaking as long as you remain faithful to me.

You surely understood me correctly. Not for a moment did I believe in the double-dealing of my Bayreuth friends, but it frightened me to know that the odious system by which everything in Bayreuth is biased by Munich, had got a footing.

On the contrary, had I given up Bayreuth I should have given up the entire undertaking. They are so grown together that so far as my great Stage Festival Play has as yet attracted attention, it is already inseparably connected with the name of *Bayreuth*.

It is gratifying to me, above all things, that you, dear friend, remain indefatigable, and that, on the whole, you seem to be convinced of the good prospects. Certainly I can see that it is going ahead about us; and I, who have such boundless patience, wish for nothing more but that we may be given plenty of *time* and not rushed. *Everything* will certainly develop; it grows and matures — only, everything must be kept *clean*.

I quite agree with your ideas in regard to the division of the necessary financial resources. More exactly expressed, it is as follows:

1. The theatre building to be considered *absolutely provisional;* it would please me if it were entirely of wood, like the gymnasiums and

Saengerfest halls: no further solidity than what is necessary to insure against collapse. Therefore economise — no ornamentation. In this building we are only giving the outline of the idea, and hand it over to the *Nation* to *perpetuate* it as a monumental structure.

2. Machinery and decorations all ideal, in relation to the inner art-work — absolutely *perfect*. *Here no* economy; everything designed for permanency, nothing temporary.

3. Singers and musicians to receive *only* compensation, but no (salary) "*payments.*" He who does not come to me from glory and enthusiasm can stay where he is. A lot of use to me a singer would be who came to me only for a silly salary! Such a person could never satisfy my artistic demands. This, my dear friend, is one of *my* miracles, by which I show to the world how a *personnel* is secured for the performance of my work; and my friends must believe in this. It is naturally quite different when a Court Intendant has to deal with such people;

then there is the very devil to pay, and it is
just this which I understand how to control. I
need about twenty leading and secondary persons; they must not cost me more than thirty
thousand thalers for the two months, or otherwise I can have nothing to do with them. A
hundred musicians, at a monthly compensation
of fifty thalers, would make at the most ten thousand thalers. *I vouch* for this, for this is *my*
empire.

It is quite different when one has to deal with
builders, carpenters, wood, canvas, lead, brushes,
and machinery: here I have no power, but can
only arrange and give orders. Here *only money*
can accomplish anything.

Further matters can be discussed quietly at
a more convenient time. I am so extraordinarily
happy to have gained a man like you as a friend,
my dear Feustel. This is more comforting for
my future than if someone were hammering and
chiselling on " my " house to-day.

Let me know when you think it necessary for

me to be in Bayreuth; I consider myself now as entirely dependent upon you. . . .

> Devotedly yours,
>
> RICHARD WAGNER.


To FRIEDRICH FEUSTEL

(LUCERNE, April 17, 1872.)

*Dear Friend!*

. . . In regard to the theatre, I repeat the following, as the result of the most mature deliberation:

The *dimensions* of the auditorium as well as of the stage must be so estimated that they may serve as the foundation of the future massive structure, for I wish to present my patrons at once with the ultimate ideal plan in a clear and distinct form. The material for the provisional building, on the contrary, must be so selected as to meet only the most necessary requirements in regard to safety.

Everything that can be economised in the way of *material* will be welcome, and in this direction

The Festival Theatre at Bayreuth

it is necessary to go to the last extreme. I consent to an entire structure of wood, however much this will vex my dear Bayreuth fellow citizens, who would like very much to see at once a building of stately exterior. In an extreme case I will adopt for the auditorium nothing more than one of those temporary structures which are so much used at present for music festivals and the like. I would even accept the obstruction of a balcony, as the entire thing is only meant to give the general idea. On the other hand, the heavy and ingenious machinery must be made thoroughly *solid;* as this, together with the foundation, shall, if God wills, outlast our lightly-put-together provisionary structure.

In short, the *material* to be reduced to a minimum. The expense which cannot be avoided *must* be met in some way. . . .

For singers, musicians, and other *personnel*, I need *not far* from one hundred thousand thalers. On this point you must have confidence in me! . . .

If, from these definite explanations, you can

feel that the purely technical authorities are sufficiently instructed for a conference, I should prefer you to get along without me, if possible, dear friend; furthermore, the telegraph wire is always there for definite questions and decisions. . . . At present my plan is to go to Vienna on the 6th of May and arrive in Bayreuth at the latest on the 15th. If I am not absolutely needed for the time being, we shall return to Lucerne the end of May, and move to Bayreuth in October with child and chattel for all time. . . .

Accept cordial greetings, dear friend, from

Yours faithfully,

RICHARD WAGNER.

To FRIEDRICH FEUSTEL

(FANTAISIE, near BAYREUTH,
May 3, 1872.)

*Dear, faithful Friend!*

. . . I am so exhausted that I shall need two days of absolute rest in order to fortify myself for the approaching period of strenuous work. Therefore I shall not leave my asylum for either to-day or to-morrow, except in case of extreme necessity; this necessity, however, is scarcely apt to arise, as our excellent burgomaster holds the key to the entire situation; you yourself could quickly take hold, and, for all musical arrangements, my splendid conductor, Hans Richter, will always be on hand.

If you have time to spare, may we hope to see you at the Fantaisie?

With the most cordial greetings,

Yours most faithfully,

RICHARD WAGNER.

No work in the entire range of musical literature had made so deep an impression upon Wagner as Beethoven's Ninth Symphony.

Through all the phases of his musical development this work remained for him the highest good, the perfection of all art; and his belief in the ultimate musical message which it contained found expression in the following words:

" There are naïve persons who continue to

write symphonies without realising that the last symphonic word was written long ago."

It was the impression created by this work, as heard at a Gewandhaus Concert in Leipzig, which determined the eighteen-year-old student of jurisprudence to follow the promptings of his heart and become a musician. In order to familiarise himself with the work, he laboriously copied the score and enthusiastically went to work on a piano arrangement. The letter in which he offers this to the publishing house of Schott in Mayence expresses the hope of " contributing in this manner to a better knowledge of this glorious Symphony. The more I familiarise myself with the great value of this work, the more depressed I am at the thought that it is so little known or understood by the greater part of our musical public."

It is a significant fact that the very first letter in the voluminous Wagner correspondence should have as its subject the Ninth Symphony of Beethoven.

During the dark days of Wagner's first visit
to Paris (1839–42), he drew one of his characteristic pen pictures of "a German musician in
Paris," who dies a lonely death with this confession of faith on his lips: "I believe in God,
Mozart, and Beethoven!"

This German musician bears strong Wagnerian
features, and the autobiographical note is emphasised by the fact that it was during this
same period of Paris privation that Wagner
again heard the Beethoven Symphony, and that
it again marked a turning-point in the musical
development of the man who was shipwrecked
in this "boundless, brilliant, dirty city." The
immediate result of this "new birth" was the
"Faust" Overture, in which the lonely artist
gave expression to his innermost thoughts and
feelings, as once the lonely Beethoven revealed
his great heart in the music of his Ninth
Symphony.

The first opportunity Wagner had for initiat-
ing the wider musical circles into the beauties

of the work came during the period of his activity in Dresden. When, in 1846, he was invited to conduct a big concert on Palm Sunday, the Ninth Symphony was the work chosen, and it was this occasion which called into existence Wagner's " programme " of the work, now considered as the most authoritative exegesis of the content. So indelible was the impression made by Wagner's earlier labour of love, that he was able to conduct all the rehearsals from memory. The performance was epoch-making in the history of the Symphony, which even by such discriminating musicians as Spohr and Mendelssohn had been pronounced the " abortive effort of a boundless fantasy."

It was but natural therefore that this monumental Symphony, which had always seemed to him the " point of transition from purely instrumental music to the art work of the future," should be chosen by Wagner to crown the ceremonies connected with the corner-stone laying on May 22, 1872.

Invitations to participate in this Beethoven Festival had been widely distributed, and the response with which they met exceeded Wagner's most sanguine expectations. Riedel's Choral Union of Leipzig and the well-known organisation which Julius Stern had called into existence in Berlin, formed the nucleus of the big chorus of three hundred singers who placed themselves at his disposal; the orchestra, composed of one hundred master musicians, at their head the ardent Wagnerian, August Wilhelmj, came from Berlin, Vienna, Munich, Leipzig, and other German cities; the solo quartette was made up of Albert Niemann, Franz Betz, Marie Lehmann, and Johanna Jackmann-Wagner. Wagner himself conducted the work, and many characteristic anecdotes have been put on record by those present. Tappert tells of the difficulty which the *Presto* of the last movement caused the Master and his men:

" Wagner expressed a desire that here all rhythms and accents should disappear and that

a flood of tone should burst in, wild and irre-
pressible. It was difficult to carry out this idea,
but after many attempts the interesting problem
was solved. When Betz got up to sing the famous
phrase, " *O friends, not these tones!* " his magnificent voice filled the auditorium, but still Wagner was not satisfied. " *With more spirit,* " he
cried, " as if you meant to say, ' What awful
rubbish you fellows are playing!' "

Bachrich, a Vienna musician who was one of
the first violinists, relates Wagner's instructions
to Henschel, the well-known kettle-drummer of
the Berlin Royal Orchestra. In the *fortissimo*
passage given to the tympani just preceding the
entrance of the Choral Finale, Wagner cried to
him excitedly: " My dear Henschel! Imagine
that the combined kettle-drums of the whole
world are to be heard in this passage. Play
away as if the devil were after you! "

An innovation which he introduced, but one
which seems not to be followed by present-day
conductors, was that of placing two smaller

choruses of men's voices, headed by Niemann and Betz, in the so-called " Trumpeters' Boxes," from which vantage-points the " Seid um-schlungen Millionen " was first heard, as if a mystery were being announced to the body of the chorus.

The idea which dominated Wagner in this performance of the Ninth Symphony was solely that of paying a tribute to the mighty genius of Beethoven. To his artists he said:

" There will be no programme, no announce-ments to be read on the street corners; we are giving no concert, only making music for our own enjoyment and to show the world how Beethoven should be played, and may the devil take him who criticises us! "

The concert at the old opera-house was pre-ceded by the ceremony of the laying of the corner-stone, the impressiveness of which event was marred by a downpour of rain. While a regimental band played the " March of Hom-age," which Wagner had written and dedicated to his royal patron, King Ludwig of Bavaria, Wagner took the hammer and gave the first three strokes, uttering the significant words: " Blessings on this stone; may it stand long and hold firmly."

On this day Wagner entered upon his sixtieth year, and all that had gone before was only a preparation for this significant moment.

From the King came a telegram, addressed to the " German poet-composer, Richard Wagner, in Bayreuth ":

From the profoundest depths of my soul I express to you, dearest friend, my warmest and most sincere congratulations on a day of such significance to all Germany. Blessing and prosperity to the great undertaking next year.

To-day more than ever, I am with you in spirit.

LUDWIG.

The chief treasures deposited under the cornerstone were this telegram and a few lines written by Wagner, which have the significant trend:

> " Hier schliess ich ein Geheimnis ein
>   Da ruh es viele hundert Jahr;
>   So lange es verwährt der Stein
>   Macht es der Welt sich offenbar." [1]

Another incident connected with this day has no artistic significance, but throws a side-light on Wagner the man. A simple Bayreuth workman in a wool factory summoned up courage to invite the man who was the subject of conversation all over Europe to act as godfather at the christening of a son born on the day of the corner-stone laying. To his joy Wagner accepted, and with his entire family appeared in the humble home, where he *remained* several hours, delighting the entire company by his high spirits and unrestrained good-humour.

[1] The writer is indebted to Henry Finck's "Wagner and His Works" for the greater part of the material used in the description of the corner-stone laying.

To Burgomaster Theodor Muncker

(Fantaisie, near Bayreuth,<br>May 25, 1872.)

*My dear Friend!*

I am too tired to come to you, and yet it distresses me not to be able to assure you immediately of the deep gratitude which I feel for your friendship and its extraordinary manifestation.

Your quiet and yet so effective efforts for the success of the splendid enterprise upon which we can now look back with satisfaction, and in all of which you showed yourself so considerate of my comfort, fills my memory as a genuine blessing from Heaven.

With my whole heart I greet you.

Your truly devoted

RICHARD WAGNER.

The Fantaisie, where Wagner and his family took up their temporary abode during the summer of 1872, was a pleasure castle built by the splendour-loving Margrave Friedrich. This monarch was the husband of the witty and intelligent Sophie Wilhelmine, the favourite sister of Frederick the Great, and her letters to her brother, though filled with scornful sarcasm, are important documents of the life and customs of the little Margravian Court in the eighteenth century.

## June, 1872–December 31, 1874.

### To Friedrich Feustel

(Fantaisie, near Bayreuth,
June 12, 1872.)

*Highly esteemed Friend!*

As you seem to have assumed the task of making my stay in Bayreuth as agreeable as possible, I beg of you to communicate the following requests to the editor of the local " Tageblatt."

The editors will be good enough to leave my name entirely out of their columns, except when it has to do with an actual report of my activity here, and about which they are able to express themselves with authority. To regale the citizens of Bayreuth with newspaper gossip from other places about me in the well-known anecdotal manner, or to report events, concerning which their own experience and exact knowledge does not justify them in forming an opinion, will prove the surest means of spoiling my life for me in Bayreuth.

My request to be spared such nonsense seems to be permissible, as I assume the obligation of giving the editors privately and truthfully all necessary information in regard to important notices. . . .

With sincere thanks for all friendliness and kind offices,

Your truly devoted

RICHARD WAGNER.

## To Emil Heckel

(Fantaisie, near Bayreuth,
June 15, 1872.)

*Dearest Friend!*

. . . As to the musicians, it is still a little early! Children, children, I have first other lambs to be looked after!

Mannheim will soon receive a souvenir from Bayreuth and

my

Humble self —

who recommends himself heartily to the Five Just Men.

## To Emil Heckel

(Fantaisie, near Bayreuth,
June 22, 1872.)

*Dear Friend!*

One cannot be too cautious! Again it has happened that I quite forgot that the person you recommended was your brother-in-law, and thus I was guilty — unintentionally — of giving you rather rude advice about a man who is related to you!

But truly, dear friend, so many questions like this come up, and as I am now always excited and engrossed with some subject, I become confused and indignant.

By the way, there is still plenty of time for the decorations! I still need two months more for my own work; then I shall look about me to the right and left in Germany, and certainly I shall also come to you in Mannheim, and God will take care of the rest.

Retain your friendship for me, and that will suffice at present for

Yours faithfully,

RICHARD WAGNER.

TO FRIEDRICH FEUSTEL

(FANTAISIE, near BAYREUTH,<br>July 3, 1872.)

*Dear Flying Dutchman of Bayreuth!*

As your ship has again come to anchor, I take advantage of this rarely favourable state of things to invite myself and my wife to dinner

on your ship (namely, at your house) to-morrow,
Thursday, at one o'clock. We beg you also to
ask Master Wölffel to join us after dinner (shall
we say — at two o'clock) with his plans for our
house. If our coming inconveniences you, I beg
of you to let me have a word from you in order
that I may keep a proper distance.

With the most cordial greetings from house
to house,

Yours faithfully,

RICHARD WAGNER.

(Also soon to be Ship's Captain.)

To JOSEPH HOFFMANN

(FANTASIE, near BAYREUTH,<br>July 28, 1872.)

*Honoured Sir!*

It is my intention to present my Stage Festival
Play, "The Ring of the Nibelung," according
to a plan which can only be realised on the one
hand by a far-reaching co-operation of the friends
of my art, and on the other by a corresponding
participation of the talent which lies scattered

in Germany for the execution of the technical part of the work.  In regard to the scenic decorations I have come to the conclusion that nothing can be attained here, worthy of the German name in its best and noblest sense, if the required task is left to our regular theatre decorators.  It is most important that we should be able to lay before the cleverest or most experienced decorative painters, sketches by genuine artists, in order that the *former* may be inspired to an idealising of their work.

I have already addressed myself to several artists (historical painters).  My attention has recently been called to your unusual work, esteemed sir, which seems to approach very nearly my requirements.  As a result of this, I feel justified in making the request that you will consider it worth your while to acquaint yourself with my poem, " The Ring of the Nibelung," to such an extent that it would be easy for you to draw such sketches of the chief scenes, as well as the setting of the same and the characterisation of the dramatic figures, as would serve either you yourself (provided you would consent to assume this task) as a model for future working out, or could be turned over to such decorative painters and costumiers as would then have to be chosen.

For the present it is sufficient to have called your attention in general to the matter, and as soon as you give me the pleasure of hearing from you I hope to find an opportunity of coming to an agreement as to further details with you personally.

The first thing is to thank you for the gratifying assurances on your part which were conveyed to me by Herr Scharf, and I remain until later

Yours very faithfully,

RICHARD WAGNER.

## To Carl Brandt

(Bayreuth, October 7, 1872.)

*Valued Friend and Associate!*

I hope that within the next few days Hoffmann will make an appointment for a meeting here in Bayreuth, and I beg you earnestly not to leave me alone with him, as that would defeat the entire purpose (of our conference).

I should like the meeting to take place by the 12th of the month; as soon as he fixes a day, I shall telegraph you and beg of you (to leave) the time free for eventual disposition in this matter.

With respectful greetings,

Yours,

Richard Wagner.

## To Carl Brandt

(Bayreuth, October 22, 1872.)

*Valued Friend and Associate!*

. . . On October 31 the contracts are to be granted. . . . I beg of you with all my might and main to be present. It is no small matter to be obliged to dispense with you in any question connected with our undertaking; you are the head and support of the entire performance. . . . For the execution of this undertaking,[1] we shall have to rely upon lucky inspirations, and these you alone have, while from other quarters I fear only reluctance and unwillingness. Therefore my urgent request of you to come here. I will also write to Hoffmann to-day! The man does not displease me in spite of the ponderousness which makes him tiresome now and then. If, in addition to his deep understanding of the matter, he really paints well, there is hope for us. We find no talent quite ready for us; we shall have to bring it to maturity.

With the most cordial greetings,

Yours very faithfully,

RICHARD WAGNER.

Malinda von Meysenburg, who is known in German letters as "The Beautiful Idealist," was

[1] A hall for the painters.

a frequent guest in Bayreuth, and one of her visits coincided with that of Brandt and Hoffmann, of whom she writes:

"We have had Brandt and Hoffmann here, and the latter submitted his sketches for the scenery of the ' Nibelung Ring.'

" The Master was pleasantly surprised and very much satisfied with them; they are the work of a genuine artist, who has grasped the idea of the poem with deep understanding and given it the setting worthy of Wagner's intentions. Whenever a slight difference of opinion occurred, and the composer with his poetic intentions in view was obliged to require this or that sacrifice of the plastic artist, this was always done with the greatest tact.

"We had here an example of what is to be realised by the ' art work of the future,' the union of all the arts into one harmonious whole, without undue emphasis being given to one or the other."

To Friedrich Feustel

(Bayreuth, November 9, 1872.)

*My dear, good Friend!*

With some concern I think of the last day we were together. The chief cause of our tacit anxiety is now removed; God knows what confusion there (Vienna) prevented timely explanation, but finally Kapka announces from Vienna that sixteen thousand florins will be ready for us within the next few weeks, and twenty thousand florins at Easter. Although the most cautious promises were made in this connection (I know for certain that already more has been collected), this will suffice to convince friend Muncker that he is justified in granting the necessary contracts. The further information which I had from him forms a new incentive for me to start on my travels as soon as possible, in order to be able to report the condition of our affairs upon the spot. I hope I shall have only good to report, and this all the more as I have resolved to work energetically everywhere in procuring the necessary funds.

Under these circumstances and with these intentions nothing remains for me to-day, on the eve of my departure, but to send you my most cordial greetings, and to repeat the assurance that your love and friendship count for very much with me, and that my gratitude for your assistance so active and effective in all directions will never be diminished.

From my whole heart,

Yours,

RICHARD WAGNER.

# TOUR OF INSPECTION

On November 10, 1872, Wagner, accompanied by his wife, started out on what he called a "tour of inspection," which meant a visit to the various German opera houses in search of material for his first production of the "Ring."

That he did this not without misgivings is to be seen from a line in one of his letters: "I must now have a look at the singers of Germany. . . . What shall I not learn? ? ? *Sighs!*"

He had been so long absent from Germany that he had got quite out of touch with operatic conditions, and it was necessary for him to establish again a point of personal contact. The conditions with which he met were on the whole discouraging, and he did not hesitate to beat a precipitate retreat from any performance which did not meet with his approval, a course

which naturally increased the number of his
enemies.  In Frankfort he attended a performance of Meyerbeer's " Prophet," and found that
" the presentation of such a Meyerbeer opera in
our larger and smaller theatres is the most non-
sensical and undignified procedure that a tortured
fantasy can imagine, and the worst of it is the
stupid seriousness with which the most ridiculous
things are accepted by a gaping public."

In Darmstadt he was present at a performance
of Auber's " The Mason," but was so indignant
that he abruptly left the house and thus, as he
expressed it, " stamped himself as a barbarian
in the eyes of the management."

In Mannheim he was the guest of Emil Heckel,
the chief of his " just men," and in the latter's
music room a circle of the elect were allowed to
listen to one of Wagner's incomparable readings
of the " Götterdämmerung."

He knew enough of hearsay to expect to find
his own works misrepresented and mutilated, and
had partially steeled himself with resignation to

meet this state of affairs. But in spite of this a much abbreviated performance of his " Fliegender Holländer " in Mannheim so excited his indignation that he left the theatre oblivious of the applause intended for the composer.

In Carlsruhe he found that the big festival scene in the second act of " Tannhäuser " was presented in such a manner " as to give the knights and ladies of honour the appearance of executing a *chassé croisé* of the contra-dance."

Everywhere he was obliged to listen to fragments of his works lustily played by the regimental bands; but this was accepted by him with fortitude, when the necessity for this was made clear to him as an impetus to his cause.

From Mayence he writes: " Music corps to the front of us, music corps to the rear of us — all blowing the Bayreuth horn!"

In Mayence he also made the acquaintance of his publisher, Franz Schott, and attended a " Fidelio " performance, which, on the whole, met with his approval.

In Cologne he grew sarcastic over a performance of Mozart's " Magic Flute " because at the entrance of the " Queen of the Night " an indifferent stage management had neglected to shift the scene from bright daylight to darkness.

A visit to Cologne was like taking the war into the enemy's country on account of the influence exerted by Ferdinand Hiller, an ardent non-Wagnerian.  Glasenapp relates a delightful episode which occurred at a banquet given in his honour here.  " A military band was stationed in a neighbouring balcony to play the ' Tannhäuser ' Overture as an act of homage to the distinguished composer.  This was followed by the ' Freischütz ' Overture of Carl Maria von Weber, during the performance of which the Master was noticed moving about uneasily in his chair.  Suddenly he sprang up, and before his surprised neighbours at the table knew what he was about, he stood in the midst of the players. At a sign from the director the music ceased and all the musicians arose.

" ' Gentlemen,' began Wagner, after apologis-
ing for the interruption, ' I have heard this overture under the bâton of the composer himself
and have preserved his traditions, particularly
the interpretation of the latter part.  If you will
permit me, I shall show you this, for your
future performances of this composition.'

" He seized the bâton, indicated the passage,
and had it played a number of times.  The young
musicians, as in a dream, hung upon his every
motion, and never forgot the evening when the
great German Master, who until then had been
only a gigantic mythical figure to them, had conducted their performance in person! "

Wagner embodied the impressions he had
gained during this tour of inspection in a paper
on " A Survey of the Present Condition of German Opera," which appeared in the Leipzig
" Musikalisches Wochenblatt."

After spending the Christmas holidays with
his family in Bayreuth, he again fared forth,
accompanied as ever by his faithful wife, to look

about him in North Germany. In a banquet given in his honour in Dresden he said:

" I declare that my sole support is in the artists! If I still cherish any hope it is not in those who *talk* about art but those who of a truth *practise* it — the musicians and the singers. I know that I can make myself understood by them everywhere."

In. regard to his Bayreuth project he said: " I cannot make my work a ' national ' one; that must be left to others, to the scattered friends of my art."

Incidentally he conducted a few concerts, but this he always did reluctantly.

" I have an aversion amounting to bitterness against concert-giving and I simply cannot expose myself to the tremendous strain, however necessary each thousand thalers to be gained in this way is to the success of our undertaking."

From Dresden he went to Berlin, where, in the presence of an exclusive audience composed of the aristocracy and *haute finance* of the Prussian

capital, he gave a reading of his " Götterdämmerung " text.

This reading was so coloured by Wagner's
personality, by his running commentary on his
views in general as to the opera, and his ideas
as to the significance of the dialogue, that the
effect upon the audience was electrifying, and the
concrete result of his Berlin visit was twenty
Patrons' Certificates.

In Hamburg he was received with as much
honour as a visiting monarch, and here he gave
a memorable performance of Beethoven's Fifth
Symphony.

After a visit to Schwerin, where he succeeded
in interesting the Grand Duke in the Bayreuth
enterprise, he returned to Berlin to conduct a
concert arranged by the Wagner Society — an
event which the anti-Wagnerian party tried in
every way to prevent from being a success.

The Intendant of the Royal Opera House,
Herr V. Hülsen, the father of the present in-
cumbent of this influential position, when ap-

proached in regard to securing the Opera House
for the concert, answered that: "It was not customary to allow the Royal Opera House to be
used for a private concert. This he could do
only by the special permission of the Emperor,
and he did not feel justified in approaching His
Majesty with such a request, as, with all due
recognition of the artistic ability of Richard
Wagner, he would nevertheless hesitate about
showing such unusual consideration to this
composer."

The conductor of the Berlin Symphony Orchestra dismissed three of his men who had taken
part in the Wagner concert. But in spite of this
opposition in high places, the concert was a
memorable musical event! The Emperor, the
Empress, and the entire court were present, and
such enthusiasm had never before been witnessed
in Berlin. Upon their return to Bayreuth Frau
Wagner wrote in a letter: "Yesterday your uncle
sadly remarked that of all the persons whom he
has now won for his cause, who run to his con-

certs and become patrons out of a feeling of personal sympathy, not one really comprehends his work, and that he himself is the only one who understands and can defend his ideas. . . .

"This splendid isolation, which your uncle feels at times, has always compelled my love from the very first; I cannot always comprehend his intentions and his ability to execute them,[1] and often ask myself which power will prove stronger in the end — his, or that of the world in which he lives!"

## To FRIEDRICH FEUSTEL

(DARMSTADT, November 20, 1872.)

*My dear Friend!*

Are you at home? How are you? In good spirits? — or otherwise? I have now swallowed four theatres and have unfortunately been obliged to participate in many gala dinners and friendly meals. Up to the present I have only one singer as definite booty, and this one, in fact,

---

[1] In the original, "Wollen und Können."

here in Darmstadt; she is of great (if as yet unknown) excellence. This evening a festival banquet by the Wagner Society! — Heckel will report to you in a few days from Mannheim his financial condition and announce himself ready to make payments at any time. Notifications of Patrons' Certificates I shall announce to you next time. I shall labour zealously — in fact, probably conduct a concert in Hamburg. To-morrow I shall be in Stuttgart. From Basel we then go — through Mayence (Wiesbaden), first to Cologne, with Aix-la-Chapelle, Düsseldorf, etc. At all events, we shall return from our first excursion before Christmas for a short time to our dear Bayreuth. (I would gladly give, as a Christmas present to anyone who could have relieved me from this trip, all the honours and festivities which have fallen to me.)

How is everything going on *at home?* Are all well and healthy in the *Fäustelei?* Is Muncker merry? And our dears? Do you three dear friends, who constitute our new home, think kindly of us? I hope so, and in this hope remain — to you and yours — your faithful grateful friend,

RICHARD WAGNER.


To FRIEDRICH FEUSTEL

(WIESBADEN, November 29, 1872.)

*My dear Friend!*

Briefly, greetings, thanks, and other things!

I visited the Grand Duke of Baden, and believe I have accomplished something by so doing. Be so kind as to send the Grand Duke directly in my name (as I promised him) the recent report (of which copies are still to be had?), as well as our earlier printed circulars with one (or more?) Patrons' Certificate, and enclose also the photograph of the theatre which is now ready.

The Societies of Darmstadt and Mayence have surprised and delighted me, and there was no lack of regimental music in the streets. You will soon receive a more accurately specified suggestion from me as to what I consider the right course to take with the societies. . . . It has to do with an appeal to the societies for more vigorous measures in order to secure the necessary results by the end of January. . . .

We travel in all directions, grow very fatigued, but shall manage to hold out.  After Cologne, Aix-la-Chapelle, Düsseldorf, Hanover, Bremen, Braunschweig, Cassel, in order that we may merit a quiet Christmas in Bayreuth with the children and our dear friends.  At New Year we start out again for a long time!

Cordial greetings to you, the family and friends!

Yours,

RICHARD WAGNER.

TO FRIEDRICH FEUSTEL

(BAYREUTH, January 14, 1873.)

*Dear Friend!*

Just returned home, I receive through Frau von Schleinitz the news that a draft for

*500 Pounds Sterling*

from the Khedive of Egypt is on the way for
Patrons' Certificates, which I wished to announce
to you, in order to restore your good spirits.

Your faithful

RICHARD WAGNER.

To CARL BRANDT

(BAYREUTH, February 16, 1873.)

*My highly esteemed dear Friend and Associate!*

If I remain silent so long, must you also let
nothing be heard from you? As far as I am
concerned, I require a great deal of good news
from you. You have heard, no doubt, how tormented I was? Finally, I was obliged to start
out on a predatory excursion in order to keep
our administrative council afloat at all hazards.
In this respect the expedition to the North has
done much good and opened up to us significant
sources of assistance. At present I am letting
my back heal from the scourging it has received,
in order to resign it to the executioner again in
March!

But now one thing! Can you not get after Brückwald energetically and induce him to furnish us with the interior of the theatre according to our recent decisions? It makes me, and also others, appear ridiculous to be able only to show to parties interested in our theatre the very uninteresting exterior, but not the interior for which all are eagerly waiting. I wish very much to have this, as I should like to use it as an engraving in connection with a little treatise of mine on the construction of theatres.

Do take the architect soundly in hand! . . . God bless you, my dear friend, you "pillar of my temple!"

Cordial greetings to the excellent committee of the Wagner Society. They were the first — then the matter went further! — and may they collect much money; I hope soon to accomplish miracles!

Your faithful *compagnon* and *associé*,

RICHARD WAGNER.

## To Friedrich Feustel

(Bayreuth, February 18, 1873.)

*Oh! my Friend!*

It is really audacious of you to pretend to live in Bayreuth! One should come here in order to be sure that he has come to the only place where you are not!

Well, I am not much better myself, either at present or in the future. Therefore — no reproaches!

And herewith — to business!

. . . Herr Nettke claims that the rich banker, Emile Erlanger in Paris, has declared his intention of giving ten thousand thaler for Bayreuth! . . . Erlanger, who has clearly shown himself very devoted to me, is said to be frightfully rich now. We should bestir ourselves seriously in securing the co-operation of this man.

And when are you coming back? You will not find me particularly recovered; it was a terrible strain on me this time. However — what must be — let it come! Farewell, and remain true to your faithfully devoted *compagnon*,

RICHARD WAGNER.

On my way back from Austria, about the end of March, I intend to stop in Munich for a few days — to the consternation of this and that person? !

The Baron Erlanger mentioned in the above letters was the financier recommended by Slidell (at that time Special Envoy to the Court of France from the Confederate government) as a suitable person for bringing out the Confederate loan in 1862.

The finances of the new Confederacy were in a bad state, there were heavy debts in Europe, and unless the bills were paid there would be an end of supplies. England was suffering for cotton, and the time seemed propitious for the successful negotiation based on this commodity.

To FRIEDRICH FEUSTEL

(BAYREUTH, July 22, 1873.)

*Dear and valued Friend!*

I informed the Burgomaster yesterday that I wished that the festivities connected with the house-raising of our theatre (which are set for Saturday) might be extended to include the highly deserving local Wagner Society. I have it at heart to introduce myself to them on this occasion and to express my thanks to them. Will you give the matter the necessary consideration?

Possibly notice of this outside of Bayreuth could be made in good time through four leading newspapers, and in that way furnish welcome intelligence to many friends and patrons who have in view a visit to Bayreuth.

Cordial greetings from

Your grateful and devoted

RICHARD WAGNER.

To Carl Brandt

(Bayreuth, August 4, 1873.)

*Esteemed Colleague!*

. . . Our *Hebefest* was very delightful and favoured by glorious weather; I—almost thought you would find your way to us this day! Liszt, my wife, and children were with me on the roof. Good spirits prevailed.

May God bless your *entrevue* with Hoffmann! Be faithful to me and — if you are always on the wing — don't forget your faithful friends in Bayreuth!

Yours cordially,

Richard Wagner.

The devotion of Liszt to his aristocratic friend, Princess Wittgenstein, had led him to accede to her wishes and hold himself aloof from Wagner even at such decisive moments as the laying of the corner-stone. The Princess, in her wish to guard jealously the musical reputation of her lover, had denied the great genius of Wagner,

Wagner and his Friends

and had frustrated the overtures made by the latter for a meeting.

But Wagner had a strong personal affection for Liszt, in addition to the gratitude he owed him as artistic sponsor of his works, and persisted in his efforts to remove the restraint of many years' standing by taking advantage of Liszt's yearly visit to Weimar to resume friendly relations.

Together with his wife, he spent three delightful days in Weimar, and, the ice once broken, the friendship of the two great composers was never allowed to suffer another interruption. Liszt paid yearly visits to Bayreuth, and it was here that he died and was buried on July 31, 1886.

Liszt's first visit after this period of estrangement was timed to coincide with the festivities connected with the " house-raising " of the new Festival Theatre. According to an old German custom, this is primarily a *fête* of the workmen, and Wagner, who with his family and Liszt formed a group on the roof, made a speech in verse in which humorous reference was made to his trusty band of co-workers and manual assistants.

## To Friedrich Feustel

(BAYREUTH, August 8, 1873.)

*Dear Friend!*

. . . I cannot leave the house for three days for the following reason. The King of Bavaria expects a dedicatory gift from me on every birthday; a year ago I was able to send him the third act of " Götterdämmerung " in manuscript; this time I should have had nothing had I not been able to use for this purpose the edition of my complete writings which is just ready.

Therefore I instructed my publisher to deliver into my hands by the 20th of August a copy *de luxe* of the ninth volume in order that it might be bound and sent off to Munich in good time. This has been promised me, only under the explicit condition, however, that I return the proofs immediately. In addition to this, I have just received a letter from the Court Councillor, Düfflipp, in which the King reminds me that he expects something from me. . . ."

These nine volumes of " Complete Writings " were sent to King Ludwig accompanied by a poem comparing them to the Sibylline books of ancient Rome:

> " Neun Bücher bot dem Konig Roms Sibylle
> Neun biet ich Dir; erfülle sie Dein Wille!"

### To Emil Heckel

(BAYREUTH, September 19, 1873.)

*Dear Friend Heckel!*

He who is once just will always remain so. Accept thanks for your friendly information. Louis XIV said to Jean Bart, " I could wish for five hundred persons like you! " Whereupon he answered, " Sire, I can well believe that! "

You could make the same answer if I wished for a dozen Heckels with his just companions in Germany.

As to the rest, you are all peculiarly exacting

people! And you really think you must warn me explicitly against accomplishing my purpose by means of a joint stock company. Is that all then my circular meant? Now, God knows! I did n't so understand it; whatever I may have hinted at in this respect was only with a view to humiliating the Germanic public! It was again a most unpleasant experience to find that the whole thing had been given to our beloved press even before I had received the slightest notice from anyone to whom the circular had been sent. What kind of people are my patrons! To run immediately to the newspapers with everything, as if it had only been gotten up for that purpose!

Now, you will have to go to work to undo this mischief in whatever way you think best, and you will have done a good deed. In the future I shall be more guarded; the public can write and gossip — also give hundreds and thousands of suggestions. But to do something — that only the " just men " do!

The chief thing is that we soon come to an agreement regarding a renewed attempt in the matter; subscription lists must be printed and sent around; a few can give (let us say, for a national object) a hundred thaler; some fifty, still more twenty, and a great many ten thaler, — namely, such as could be persuaded to support so great an undertaking, without having any special interest which could determine them at any time to make the trip to Bayreuth for the purpose of being present at the performances.

You should work out a sketch for a well-organised agitation of this sort and send it to me for my approval, and then, armed with my permission, bring the matter before the people with frightful publicity, so that no one can say, " Yes, but I know nothing whatever about it " — as I meet with so often.

Well! I hope to see you here soon! I shall give no more concerts. They only do harm instead of inciting to further effort; everyone thinks that enough has been accomplished by these concert receipts, and then all is up with the matter. So it is with Cologne, where, as a *result of the concert*, the Wagner Society has accomplished absolutely nothing. On the whole — !

Now cordial greetings to the just men, particularly the miracle doctor, also, greetings to you and your dear wife from me and mine.

Yours

RICHARD WAGNER.

A second appeal had been sent out on August 31, 1873, stating that unless fresh help came work in the building would have to be suspended, and containing an invitation to the friends and patrons of his undertaking to be present at a conference to be held in Bayreuth October 31.

Wagner had in mind a widespread national subscription, but did not wish that either he or his council should take the initiative in the matter, but that this should be assumed by a *consortium* of wealthy and influential men.

To Friedrich Feustel

(BAYREUTH, September 30, 1873.)

*My dear Friend!*

I thank you for your renewed efforts with Wölfel; only I should like to beg you earnestly to attend in person the proposed conference, whether it takes place on Monday or Tuesday! However unjust it may be on my part to lay such strong claims upon your friendship for me, I should not know what to do without your assistance; for your consolation in the future, I promise you that I shall never have another house built for me, not even in Germany.

My circular, by the way, begins to bear good fruits. Among other things, I was touched to-day by the notification of a one-third patron in Austria, who wrote that he had sent Heckel two hundred thaler in order that he might become a *full* patron.

If a mason with a broken nose presents himself to you, with a card from me, I beg you to give him a fee of ten florins from the building fund; from the time of the corner-stone laying he has worked day after day in the building and has always impressed me favourably by his diligence and friendly attitude.

He was dismissed from work this evening and took a very decent leave.

Therefore — everything  considered — remain kind  to  your

Ever grateful

RICHARD WAGNER.


To EMIL HECKEL

(BAYREUTH, September 30, 1873.)

*Dearest Friend!*

The answer to your letter, or rather suggestion, really demands some deliberation.

I have no word to say as to the manner in which the Mannheim society deems proper to serve the purpose for which it was founded: at any rate, as it called into existence the idea of the Wagner Societies, it also has a right to take the initiative; and the honour of being the champion in this matter will be contested by no one.

Only be cautious in boasting about me; we could not count on Chicago and London quite so unconditionally; in both cities a new theatre had already been built and was to be fitted out according to my wishes — only, however, if I would assume personal control, in which case the *personnel* of the artists should be selected according to my choice. This refers to my opera in general. But we now come to the decisive point: in Berlin a " Wagneriana " has been formed with subscriptions already amounting to two hundred and twenty thousand thaler, and the prospect of a million is held out to me if I will transfer Bayreuth (with modifications) to Berlin; the same offer would have been immeasurably easier for Vienna than to have collected money there for Bayreuth. It is therefore not proven that my theatre would not have been built for me in a *large German metropolis;* but the vital point lies in the fact that I had in mind an undertaking for the benefit of the entire German nation in a neutral spot, and not for the people of one certain city. Cities (like Chicago, etc.) will perhaps also be found in Germany, but — the *German public* is not to be found.

In regard to the drawing up and issuing of a subscription list it would perhaps be more advisable if this were done by a *consortium* of influential men from the various German cities. In this matter I am already somewhat bound, as a rich and energetic Hamburg merchant intends to call together such a meeting for the 15th of October.

Will you not put yourself in touch with him? He wished, at all events, to communicate with you.

If you take any steps towards issuing a manifesto (which might be very effective), I shall request you to consult with Nietzsche as to its wording; at all events, you can first invite him to draw up such a manifesto. For this I have quite especial confidence in him — particularly in him . . .

I am tired, God knows, but send you and yours cordial greetings.

Yours faithfully,

RICHARD WAGNER.

An episode which should have been humiliating to Wagner's countrymen was the liberal offer made to him by Chicago.

This city wished to celebrate its renascence after the "Great Fire" of 1871 by building a theatre for Wagner, over which he was to assume the personal direction, with the liberty of choosing his own *personnel.*

This offer he was unable to accept, but the confidence in his art, which a city was ready to give, deeply touched him, and more than once, in moments of deepest depression, he referred to this offer, and often gave expression to a lingering regret that he had not taken his art work and his family to a land which held out such hospitable arms to him and his ideas.

Later he wrote: " Great Heavens! Such sums as I should have earned in America! People ought to be willing to give *me* a present, without asking in return anything more than what I am now doing, and which is the very best I am able to do."

### To Emil Heckel

(BAYREUTH, October 17, 1873.)

*My dear Friend!*

The " Conference " was again a — More about this verbally!

Let us abide by the delegates' meeting. If there are only a few of us, we at least represent something — namely, the Wagner Societies. A manifesto can very properly be issued in their name. My wife has written you concerning this.

Now, do come, and if possible bring Zeroni

with you. My opinion is that eventually everything will go well.

With the most cordial greetings,

Yours respectfully,

RICHARD WAGNER.

To BURGOMASTER THEODOR MUNCKER

(BAYREUTH, October 31, 1873.)

*Dearest Burgomaster!*

Here are sample copies of a Manifesto drawn up by Professor Nietzsche, and which I wish distributed for temporary cognisance to the delegates who have arrived and those yet to come.

Who can best look after this matter? In fact, *how* can I best learn who has arrived? (I have also to bear in mind the dinner-table, in regard to the number of covers.) At present I *know* of only Nietzsche, Heckel, Ballingad, and M. du Moulin. Unfortunately I am much embarrassed by my lack of servants.

Pardon me and remain kindly disposed toward

Yours most respectfully,

RICHARD WAGNER.

The last day of October came, and with it a number of delegates representing the Wagner Societies and the Society of Patrons.

Friedrich Nietzsche, who was one of these delegates and had brought with him the desired proclamation, wrote to a friend: " After a tour of inspection in mud, fog, and darkness, a conference was held in the city hall, when my appeal was read and politely but firmly rejected. I myself protested against any alterations, and suggested that Professor Stern be intrusted with the task of drawing up a new one. . . .

" The building is much more beautiful and well proportioned than it appears in the picture. It is impossible to look upon it without emotion, as it outlines itself against the clear autumn sky. We have a house, and that is now our symbol."

A letter written by Elizabeth Nietzsche-Foerster, the sister of the great German philosopher, contains the following allusion to this manifesto:

" At the instance of Wagner the executive board of the Wagner Societies had requested

my brother to draw up an appeal to the German
nation in aid of the Bayreuth enterprise. With
much reluctance my brother sketched it out between October 18–20, 1873, worked it out in detail, and had a number of copies printed in order
to distribute in Bayreuth. But the proclamation
was politely but firmly rejected by the delegates.
Wagner was indignant about the matter."

The Stern manifesto was printed and freely
distributed, but in spite of the vigorous tone in
which it was expressed, and the subscription lists,
which, at the suggestion of Heckel, had been
placed in every book, music, and art shop in Germany, a few thalers subscribed by some Göt-
tingen students was the total result of this broadly
outlined " National Subscription," from which so
much was expected and upon which so much
depended.

It was in reply to the discouraging reports
concerning the same that Wagner wrote to
Heckel.

To Emil Heckel

(Bayreuth, November 19, 1873.)

*O you most excellent Man!*

Accept my most heartfelt thanks for that which you are doing, and which it is not necessary to specify further! You can console yourself with the thought that if the ways and means which you are pursuing do not lead to the goal, then nothing else — of an honourable nature — would help us.

God knows, possibly you will find that much good comes even from the newspapers; I have often noticed that a lack of understanding creates more confusion than pure malice!

I go to-morrow to Munich to see if there is any hope of interposition on the part of the King.

Even if worse happens, we shall still be able to keep to the year 1875, if this winter bears good fruit! If I am able to close with Brandt and Hoffmann definitely in the spring, then they will still have time enough — according to their earlier statements — in which to get ready. I shall have a conference with both of them here, at the end of this month.

Therefore — let us hope! Through the measures which you are taking with such energetic caution, we shall learn in the end the still latent power of the German character; that is the consideration which almost outweighs the success of the undertaking itself.

A thousand cordial greetings to you and yours from me and my dear wife.

Yours,

RICHARD WAGNER.

To JOSEPH HOFFMANN

(BAYREUTH, December 19, 1873.)

*Highly esteemed Sir and Friend!*

Accept my sincerest thanks for your efforts, of which you inform me in your kind letter, and be assured that it is not until now, after having become more closely acquainted with you and your important achievements, that I feel myself relieved on the subject of the artistic success of our undertaking. Highly as I valued the news from you, I was prevented by a very special reason from letting you hear from me until later.

Even now I am not in possession of information which would permit me to feel assured of positive assistance, and without which it would seem ill-advised to adhere to the year 1875 for the performances, or to grant the contracts for the beginning of the work at the first of the year.

As I expect any day now, however, to receive this information, and which from certain signs I venture to hope will prove favourable, I must beg of you to exercise the same patience with me. As we, furthermore, have as yet only provisory information as to your conditions, permit me to notify you, on my part, that I, as well as the gentlemen of the committee, consider your demands and suggestions quite reasonable, and only in one particular will it be necessary to find some other way of satisfying you, and that is in regard to the two per cent royalty that you claim, without our first being able to discover upon what basis of receipts this percentage is to be deducted.

The performances at the Festival Theatre in Bayreuth are never to be accessible by an admission fee, nor are they to be given for the financial profit of any person. On the contrary, they are to take place, once for all, only when the costs of the same — that is, the necessary outlay and the compensation for the assisting *personnel* — shall be covered by the voluntary subscriptions of the patrons, but never is there to be a question of recompense for the author.

I believe, however, that I shall be able to comply with your wishes by pledging myself to permit such theatres as wish to present my works according to the customary admission fees, to do so only under the condition that the scenery is executed from your designs and that an agreement concerning the same is entered into with you and your heirs.

For the present, as our money has grown quite scarce, we have instructed Baron Viktor v. Erlanger in Vienna, who has pledged himself for fifteen hundred thalers, to pay this sum to you immediately as the compensation which you claim, and do not doubt that this will be done.

I have to express my sincere thanks, as well as those of my wife, for your kind souvenir and also for your obliging efforts, and at the same time to beg you to remember us both cordially to your esteemed wife whom we have not the pleasure of knowing.

With the reservation of more definite news for you shortly, I remain, with the deepest respect,

Yours,

RICHARD WAGNER.


TO EMIL HECKEL

(BAYREUTH, January 19, 1874.)

*Esteemed, dear Friend!*

It is only fitting that I should address myself to you, the most active and efficient founder and promoter of a society for the furtherance of my proposed Stage Festival Play, when a decisive step is to be taken, which can be carried into effect more suitably by an intelligent and proven friend of my undertaking, than by me, the originator of the undertaking.

Powerful assistance has become necessary, if the work we have commenced is to be carried on to speedy execution; everything depends upon despatch in this matter, as it is dependent upon the endurance of my personal vitality.

In the course of two years we have reached the point where we are provided with one hundred thousand thaler by the close friends of my art; with this money we have laid the permanent foundation of the entire undertaking by erecting a Stage Festival Play theatre, the solidity of which insures its usefulness for an immeasurable period of time. But now, just at a time when there can be no further delay in giving the definite commissions for the execution of the stage machinery and decorations, the strength of the former patrons of the undertaking is exhausted, progress is necessarily retarded, and will be forfeited to a sad fate unless some decisive power comes to its assistance.

My local counsellors are of the opinion that the undertaking should be supported at any cost, up to the point of the projected Festival performances, and that we might expect with certainty to cover the costs by the support which comes to us from all directions by those interested in this unusual enterprise. With this in view, we should only need a guarantee sufficient to insure the uninterrupted progress of the work.

In order to secure such a guarantee, I recently approached my noble benefactor, the King of Bavaria, but, for reasons quite obscure to me, he refused my request.

You know that of late we have been searching for such a guarantee among particularly sympathetic and wealthy friends. Should, however, even temporary relief grow out of this attempt, I am nevertheless resolved to look for help in

so significant a cause in the only direction which
would impart the proper dignity to the enterprise.

If I have here in mind the " Empire," you are
not unacquainted with the fact that the thought
of seeing my undertaking and the *Kulturwillens-
akt*[1] which it represents, discussed by the rep-
resentatives of our Parliament, has always filled
me with horror, because I feared that not a single
person would be discovered among all of these
who would be able to expound convincingly the
rightful significance of my undertaking and defend it against the insulting defamations of the
absolutely ignorant, but at the same time powerful, press.   On the contrary, I have now decided
to offer the first performances of my work to our
victorious Emperor, as a lustrum celebration of
the famous peace with France, closed in 1871.
The chief thing would be to place the performance of my " Nibelung " work — which is constructed on entirely new lines corresponding
more closely to the peculiarities of the German

[1] Voluntary deed of culture.

character — in sharp contrast with the theatrical performances with which, according to a somewhat reprehensible custom, such solemn days are usually commemorated. I venture to think that should my offer be accepted, it would express the recognition of a significant epoch in German culture. I could not be expected to express myself forcibly and convincingly on this subject; I must unconditionally look among the friends of my art, or the patrons of my undertaking, for an advocate who, armed with the detailed instructions which I have drawn up as a guide, would be able to present my project in its true significance and in a favourable light before the proper personages.

In this, as well as in other matters, it fills me with pleasant encouragement to appoint you, dear and valued friend, as my choice for the position of chief mediator with your own sovereign, the Grand Duke of Baden, whom I so highly esteem. It was this model German prince who received me and my artistic undertakings with such truly enlightened favour when in 1861, after long ban-

ishment, I again put my foot upon German soil.
Since that time I have had no cause to complain
of any diminution in the high-hearted sentiments
which greeted me at that time, and believe therefore that you will find His Royal Highness seriously prepared and favorably disposed, if you
approach him with a request for assistance along
the lines I have already indicated, in the name
of all those who have already given their support to my cause, — among whom I count with
peculiar satisfaction my royal patron himself.

It would not be fitting for me to suggest further
measures for the pursuance of this course; if,
however, the Grand Duke should declare himself
in our favour, it is to be taken for granted that
the co-operation of His Royal Highness the
Crown Prince of Germany would naturally occur
at once to my Illustrious Highness as the most
effective. I should only permit myself to suggest
that the Grand Dukes of Saxon Weimar and
Mecklenburg, as well as the Duke of Nassau, all
of whom have already taken a great personal

interest in my undertaking, should eventually be secured as co-operators.

If I now specify exactly what I anticipate as the crowning result of all my wishes and efforts in behalf of my undertaking, it would be to secure herewith a commission from the German Emperor for three complete performances of my Stage Festival Play, the " Ring of the Nibelung," during the summer of 1876, at the Festival Theatre erected for this purpose in Bayreuth, as a first lustrum celebration of the peace made with France.

In return for this, the sum of one hundred thousand thalers — in other words, a third of the total cost — should be guaranteed in support of the undertaking. . . .

As it would not be a difficult task to specify in plain figures the number of seats which rightfully would need to be put at the disposal of the donors of such a sum, I refrain, in this communication, from any amplification of the business aspect of the matter, and beg of you, in conjunction with our valued friends in Mannheim, to take the first steps toward the realisation of the idea which I have in mind, and which, I freely admit, originated with you.

With devoted friendship,

Yours faithfully,

RICHARD WAGNER.

Wagner had already appealed to his royal patron, King Ludwig of Bavaria, but his letter had remained unanswered.

In spite of this, however, he was convinced of the genuine interest and sympathy of the King, and went to Munich to make personal inquiry as to the strange silence. A conference with the King's councillor, Düfflipp, had no immediate results, and after a period of anxious waiting Wagner asked for a decisive answer, be it Yes! or No!

Promptly the annihilating telegram came that the King refused the guarantee. Heckel was at once summoned and found Wagner in a state of

despair: " I shall board up the sides of the Festival Theatre in order to prevent the owls from
nesting there until we are able to resume work
on the building."

The secret ground of King Ludwig's momentary displeasure with his favourite was that
Wagner had refused to furnish a setting to an
extremely weak poem, which in Latin verse ex-
tolled the virtues of the Bavarian monarch, on
the plea that he was occupied in completing his
" Götterdämmerung."

Wagner was not told that it was the wish of
the King, and the latter's displeasure was fanned
into flame by the ever-ready Munich intriguers.

Feustel, to whom the secret had been imparted,
had pledged himself not to tell Wagner how matters stood, but he broke the spirit, if not the
letter, of his vow by giving the particulars to
Heckel, who was then at liberty to act as
mediator.

Later an effort was made to induce the Grand
Duke of Baden to intercede with Emperor Wil-

liam I for his consent to accept the performances as a sort of lustrum celebration of the peace following the Franco-Prussian War.

In this connection Wagner suddenly uses the date " 1876 " for the first time.

After a long wait the Prussian court returned a negative answer, which could be attributed only to a feeling of delicacy and consideration toward the Bavarian King, who was known to be jealous of any outside assistance being given to his favourite. Bismarck is reported to have said, " I do not know but that the King of Bavaria would have considered that we were poaching upon his preserves, had we advanced Wagner's efforts! "

As soon as Heckel had thrown a light on the mysterious attitude of the King, Wagner had not delayed writing to his royal patron, who in his former enthusiastic tone answered:

*" No, no, and again no! It must not end so! Something must be done! "*

The old relations were resumed between the

master and the disciple, and Wagner was able
to announce to Heckel:

"Everything is in order with His Majesty!"


## To Emil Heckel

(BAYREUTH, February 9, 1874.)

*Dear, good Friend Heckel!*

Only have courage!

And all will be well! —

The matter has been arranged with His Majesty; the undertaking in which you are taking
such a serious and splendid part is now assured.

More details soon! —

. . . I *knew* that all of that would be in vain;
a "wise fool" is necessary for my cause! — but
who is foolish nowadays? —

This in haste! More soon! With my whole
heart,

Yours,

RICHARD WAGNER.

### To Carl Brandt

(BAYREUTH, February 9, 1874.)

*Dear Friend!*

At last I have reached the point where I am able to put the direct question to you — and Hoffmann.

Provided you receive all the necessary conditions, in the form of a contract, for the beginning of your work here in Bayreuth by the end of the month, can you then be ready with everything so that we may plan for the performances with absolute certainty for August, 1875?

Even if you cannot assent to the above, a conference at the end of the month will be indispensable in order that the contracts for 1876 (should this become necessary) can be discussed.

With cordial greetings,

Yours faithfully,

RICHARD WAGNER.

## To Emil Heckel

*Dear Friend!*

The signature of the King has just come. It guarantees a credit of a hundred thousand thaler from his own private treasury, in order that the costs of the stage machinery, decorations, and lighting may be defrayed; during the period of the loan all moneys accruing from the Patron Certificates shall be credited to the Royal Treasury in liquidation of the debt, until which time all the designated acquisitions remain the property of the Royal Court Secretary.

This is the contract.

You can see that we are placed in a position to go forward, but have not as yet received any additional funds, and therefore remain, as before, dependent upon the support of the public if we are eventually to carry out our undertaking.

I beg of you, therefore, to proceed with that circumspection and caution in making your communications and notifications necessary to the two purposes:

1. To present this supervening relief only in the light of a guarantee for the realisation of the enterprise.

2. Not to make people believe that now nothing more is left for them to do.

We consider it, therefore, best simply to report the fact, namely:

That the proposed contracts with the painter Hoffmann in Vienna, as well as with the Royal Theatre machinist, Brandt, for the furnishing of the decorations and stage machinery, are to be closed as soon as possible.

I think this will be sufficient and refute everything. In the same way I shall now write to the singers I have selected, and also give instructions in regard to the orchestra, all of which will soon give another aspect to the matter.

I shall rejoice all the more if this gives you genuine pleasure, my dear friend, as I unfortunately enjoy but little of this pleasure, having been so wearied and tormented by all that has preceded that the success leaves me rather cold and mindful only of my duties.

Cordial greetings from house to house,

Yours,

RICHARD WAGNER.

To FEUSTEL AND MUNCKER

(BAYREUTH, March 7, 1874.)

*My highly esteemed Sirs and Friends!*

It will ever remain an impossibility for me to give adequate expression to my gratitude for, and recognition of, your great service in the under-taking I have initiated. This is the first thing which troubles me in responding now to your communication of to-day!

The second is that I am obliged to regard it as utterly impossible to pay my debt of deeply felt gratitude by yielding to your wish that our performances should take place in the coming year.

I thought that I had already expressed myself

quite clearly and sufficiently on this point at our last meeting, and therefore can only repeat that the more seriously I force myself to look the matter squarely in the face, the more fully I am able to estimate the injury which the delay in the contracts has caused. . . .

As a result of this delay I have got out of touch with the *personnel* I previously had in view, and am obliged to start again from the very beginning in regard to securing a new one. For example, I could not now say to any singer, " Don't make any contract for the summer, in order that you may be at my disposal," and I should regard myself as fortunate, should I be able to persuade any of the former ones to place themselves at my disposal for a few days, in addition to their other obligations.

Believe me, *it is quite impossible* to present the enormous four-part work, each part of which would require three months' preparation in the largest theatres, in the time which now remains for us, from now until next year.

That is *one* thing! The other is your suggestion and wish that the means be collected by my personal activity. Provided I *should* be successful in getting together considerable sums by constant travelling about and constant concert-giving, it grieves me to be obliged to declare to you that I could not endure the strain, and it is for this reason that I am obliged to provide myself with a conductor to assume these duties even for the Festival performances, a precaution which I was obliged to take in Munich in the past. I feel, more than either one of you, my highly esteemed friends, that the ultimate guarantee of the success of our great undertaking lies in the maintenance of my physical and mental vitality, because no one can estimate the task which I have imposed upon myself in this respect. And furthermore, my experience of the preceding year has convinced me that all these attempts to give a personal impetus to the matter in no way produce results commensurate with the effort made. On the contrary, I learned quite dis-

tinctly from the experience that it is not the
idea which is preached beforehand, but the fact
of the proposed musical performances, which
may possibly arouse a certain degree of curious
sympathy, and this eventually may procure for
us the necessary funds. On the other hand, this
sympathy can be increased by prolonging and
thus exciting curiosity, provided the one fact remains firm, and that is the eventuality of the
performances. By means of the rehearsals
which will be held in the summer of 1875, with
decorations, etc., this interest can be raised to
a profitable degree of impatience — which would
be all the better for us.

I am quite clear about this. But that about
which I am quite in the dark is, how I am to
persuade myself to invite fifteen hundred guests
(apart from my *personnel*), among them most
distinguished personalities, in the present condition of the entertaining strength of Bayreuth.
This it is, my highly esteemed friends, which
is so serious a point that I am forced to beg of

you to throw some light on the subject, which will quiet my anxieties.

I do not believe that it will be possible for you to convince me that, by the means which up to the present have been used, a thousand patrons, most of them from aristocratic circles, to say nothing of five hundred free seats, can be so accommodated in our hotels and private houses as not to convert the assembling in Bayreuth into a disagreeable experience, which would make the repetition of the Festival an impossibility the year following.

I therefore regard it as my duty, my highly valued friends, to beg of you to arrange a meeting for an early date for deliberating this very important point and as far as I am able to judge of the difficulty of the situation, you will find it by no means too early for serious consideration of the matter, if we expect to receive the guests of the Festival in a befitting manner in the summer of 1876, so that they will cherish no manifest objection to coming again in the year 1877.

May you receive this answer in a friendly and considerate manner, as the conviction of one deeply serious and also of one weighed down with cares, — for the faith's sake, — and beg of you to ascribe it to my great gratitude toward you.

With the deepest respect,

Yours,

RICHARD WAGNER.

Among the visitors at the first Festival in 1876 was the great Russian composer, Tschaikowsky, who was at that time only thirty-six years of age. In a letter written to an intimate friend, and since published, he expressed himself unreservedly as to the impressions he had received at Bayreuth.

" Bayreuth is an insignificant little city, in which several thousand persons are gathered together. As far as accommodations are concerned, one is very badly served. We had ordered our room beforehand and that is very nice, but the first day I succeeded in getting my dinner only by the greatest effort, and yesterday's breakfast I owe only to a lucky accident.

" . . . I am not at all bored, but, on the other hand, I cannot say that my stay here gives me any great pleasure, so that all my thoughts and wishes are directed toward fleeing from here as soon as possible and returning to Russia *via* Vienna."

From Henry T. Finck we also have an account of the material discomfort to which the guests were subjected, but, unlike Tschaikowsky, his musical enthusiasm enabled him to take a humourous view of the situation:

" The chief difficulty was to get something to eat. The small hotels could accommodate only their own guests, and of restaurants there were only a few. I remember a characteristic scene at Lochmüller's, the principal restaurant at that time. Everyone at the crowded tables was imploring the waiters to serve them, and finally the majority decided that they might save an hour or two by waiting on themselves. So they all crowded around the buffet, ready to grasp whatever appeared from the kitchen; while the waiters, pushed aside, stood in a corner, and one of them sarcastically suggested to his companions that they should sit down and let the guests wait on them."

## To Emil Heckel

(BAYREUTH, April 17, 1874.)

*Esteemed Friend!*

Best thanks! We are now burdened with the arrangements of our house and our approaching move. My wife suffering continually with a cold, and I — expecting good things and — putting up with bad. I expect Richter the beginning of May to assist me for four months. He will then see about your tenor. . . .

I shall not lack for men, but I have not many women to boast of. The summer will make all this clear; just at present I still have winter somewhat in my bones!! . . .

Most cordial greetings to you and the friends from

Yours faithfully,

RICHARD WAGNER.

In addition to Wagner's anxieties in regard to the building of the theatre were connected those of his private residence, to which, in jest, he gave the name of " Argersheim " (The House of Anger), as a play upon his " Nibelheim " of the " Ring." He had so often had to call upon Feustel to adjust difficulties with the architect that he wrote: " For your consolation in the future, I promise you that I shall *never* build another house, not even in Bayreuth."

The first object which greets the eye of the visitor to Wahnfried is a life-sized bronze bust of Wagner's royal patron, which was put in place during the rehearsals of 1875, and stands as an enduring symbol of the loyal protection offered by a German monarch to a German composer.

The house is singularly simple in its decorative scheme, with the exception of the semicircular space over the entrance, which is occupied by *sgraffitto* painting of an allegorical character.

It represents the German myth, which, in the person of Wotan the Wanderer, in mantle and wide-brimmed hat drawn down over his missing eye, journeys through the world accompanied by his ravens. The features are those of Ludwig Schnorr von Carolsfeld, the creator of the *rôle* of " Tristan." The Wanderer meets on his journeyings the figure of Tragedy, bearing the features of Wilhelmine Schröder-Devrient, the great dramatic singer, and a second figure in which the art of Music is personified by Frau Cosima Wagner. She leads towards Wotan the boy Siegfried (Siegfried Wagner), who with his self-forged sword is symbolic of the Art Work of the Future.

Below the picture is the reddish marble tablet bearing the name of the house " Wahnfried," flanked on either side by the explanatory inscription: "Hier, wo mein Wahnen Frieden fand, Wahnfried sei dieses Haus von mir genannt."

In this house Wagner spent the happiest decade of his life with his wife Cosima and three children. Villa Wahnfried became the amplified fulfilment of the yearning to which he gave expression in an earlier letter to Uhlig: "I want a small house with meadow and garden! To work with zest and pleasure! Rest! Rest! Rest! Country! Country: a cow, a goat. Then health — happiness — hope!"

### To Joseph Hoffmann

(Bayreuth, June 9, 1874.)

*Esteemed Sir and Friend!*

I wish to express to you my sincere thanks for the alterations in your beautiful designs. Thereby the room of Hunding has become thoroughly in keeping with the demands of the dramatic action, and it is so excellent that I cannot find that it has forfeited anything of its character. No less have I to thank you for the space in front of the hall of the " Gibichung " on the banks of the Rhine.

The general effect will be magnificent; it is to be hoped that the level space of the front and middle stage is wide enough to accommodate the great number of persons required by the action which takes place here.

One wish I have always had, namely, to see the entrance of the hall in somewhat more of a straight or curved profile; here the decisive meeting of the chief catastrophe takes place. I have made the mistake of keeping, unconsciously, in view our — very incorrect — theatrical conventionalities, according to which, for example in " Lohengrin," the portal of the minster is placed sufficiently to one side so that for a long time the action could take place on the steps.

This time I should like to have a concession on your part, according to which you would move the entire scene rather more from right to left, so that more would be seen of the hall and somewhat less of the Rhine.

In this way:

(In the original is a drawing indicating this.)

from which we assume that we have here only a landing place on the river, while in the first and last act we look out upon the broad stream itself.

But it will be difficult for you to sacrifice anything here, for the picture, as you have given it, is unusually characteristic and beautiful.

Be indulgent and remain favourably disposed always to yours

Very faithfully,

RICHARD WAGNER.

TO CARL BRANDT

(BAYREUTH, June 9, 1874.)

*Dear Friend!*

I am in trouble, which I pour out to you as a friend!

Frau Jaide troubles me. If she had only come **to** me at the right time instead of going off to Vienna to introduce herself as a Wagner singer!

That she "injured" herself in Vienna signifies nothing, absolutely nothing, although I wish she had considered herself as one of my chosen artists and not subjected herself to the risks of a Vienna appearance.

This corresponds to her character, which I could wish were more serious, so that she should more deeply realise the nature of the great task before her.

From inquiries which I have made from absolutely reliable authorities and disinterested friends, one thing seems certain: Frau Jaide is credited with a big talent, a highly significant artistic instinct as a dramatic interpreter, and a warm noble nature but — her voice is said to have been injured, she is said to have grown unreliable, and therefore does not fulfil in the performance the expectation she arouses in the rehearsals.

For me this is *no* small matter — during the

time which Frau Jaide tardily allows to go by — presumably in Vienna appearances — to be obliged to decide about the casting of the chief *rôles* in my work.

Now I beg of you! You are in Darmstadt on the spot; tell me something of the assiduity of this singer. Do you consider her as thoroughly reliable as the mainstay of my performances should be?

I most heartily hope that you will be able to quiet my mind on this point!

As stage machinist you are now obliged to help me by deed and word in everything. Do you remember that I also applied to you for information about your orchestra? ? ? . . .

May Fate be treating you particularly well, but — always think a little of

Yours cordially and faithfully,

RICHARD WAGNER.

Frau Jaide was the Darmstadt singer whom Wagner discovered on his tour of inspection and mentioned in his letter to Feustel as " the only singer whom I have as definite booty so far — she is of great (if as yet unknown) excellence."

In March, 1874, Wagner wrote to her as follows: " I am now at the point where I can request you to come to Bayreuth for a long stay, in order to afford me the opportunity of acquainting you with the great task which I hope to see accomplished by means of your great gifts.

" Come when you will, and when it best suits your convenience; during the course of the summer I expect similar visits from all of the other artists whom I have chosen."

At first Wagner hoped that Frau Jaide might answer for *Sieglinde,* but later he was obliged to abandon this idea and intrust to her the *rôles* of *Erda* and *Waltraute.*

## To Friedrich Feustel

(BAYREUTH, June 10, 1874.)

*Dear Friend!*

Every evening my musicians are with me in order to be coached in the proper interpretations of my scores, which the singers are soon to begin studying with them.

He who wishes to participate in these gatherings is heartily welcome, even were it the highly esteemed " circle." Every night something is going on, and I cannot leave the house a single evening.

Faithful greetings from your ever grateful friend,

RICHARD WAGNER.

The summer of 1874 was devoted to studying the big score with the young musicians of the so-called " Nibelungkanselei," presided over by Dr. Hans Richter. Among the young " copyists " who were at work under his direction were Anton Seidl, Joseph Rubinstein, and Franz Fischer.

Chests were already filled with the different parts of the score, and every evening some part of the gigantic work was taken out and gone through with, and here was laid the foundation of the " Bayreuth style."

None of these young disciples was more thoroughly imbued with the spirit of the work than Anton Seidl, who was afterward to become the great Wagner prophet of America. Later Wagner wrote of him: " At any moment I could, had it been necessary, have intrusted him with the direction of the entire work. He was filled with the spirit of the ' Nibelung Ring ' from the crown of his head to the soles of his feet!"

To CARL BRANDT

(BAYREUTH, June 14, 1874.)

*Esteemed Friend!*

I should like to have a list of the

*Most Meritorious,*

consequently

the most *excellent,* musicians

of the grand Ducal Court Orchestra. To whom shall I apply? . . .

I should like you to ask whichever conductor of the orchestra you consider most capable of deciding this point, an opinion which will be treated with the most absolute confidence. Out of six orchestras, which are unemployed during these months, I intend to form my big orchestra. . . .

With the most cordial greetings,

Yours faithfully,

RICHARD WAGNER.

### TO JOSEPH HOFFMANN

(BAYREUTH, October 12, 1874.)

*Honoured Sir and Friend!*

It is not my *wish* that you withdraw from further co-operation in the execution of the plans which you have designed. I have demonstrated to you that it was most important to me, for the successful progress of the work, to keep you on good terms with the gentlemen to whom the execution of your plans was directly intrusted. At the present moment it is not my purpose to inquire closely into the reasons which have arisen for making impossible this necessary unanimity. It is sufficient to assume that you yourself recognise that the situation has grown impossible. This opinion I have imparted to the gentlemen of the Executive Council, without, however, expressing a *wish*. My sole, sincere desire is that you and I, two honourable men, should part in peace for the present. In regard to the payment of any indemnification, this question belongs to a province in which I take part with all the necessary force and energy only when it concerns the accomplishment of my undertaking as a whole, and as I have eliminated any idea of material profit for myself, I leave all decisions of this nature to the directors of the economic part of the undertaking, who are pledged to the strictest economy on every point.

As soon as the part Herr Brückner is to take in the final execution of the decorations is settled, I promise you without fail to remember him and also yourself by compensating you for the part you have taken in the matter by the further protection of your copyright in the future.

With the request that you present my regards

to your highly esteemed wife and mother-in-law,
I extend my hand to you at parting and remain
always

Yours respectfully,

RICHARD WAGNER.

During a long stay with Brandt in Darmstadt
Hoffmann had finished the models for the
scenery of the " Ring "; but serious differences
of opinion had occurred between himself and his
colleagues, as a result of which the scenic execution of his models had been entirely transferred to the Brückner brothers in Coburg, and
Brandt appointed exclusively to the task of in-
specting their work.

To CARL BRANDT

(BAYREUTH, NOVEMBER 23, 1874.)

*Dear Herr Brandt!*

Can you not at last see that my wish in regard to the orchestra affair is looked after by
the suitable person in the Darmstadt Orchestra? ? ?  I only need this information in order

to form my orchestra *temporarily, whereupon I can only then* take the official steps.

Yesterday I finished my score, and shall devote myself now entirely to business.

Cordial greetings from

Yours very faithfully,

RICHARD WAGNER.

The score of the "Götterdämmerung" was finished in November, 1874.

"Finished in Wahnfried. I say nothing further. R. W." he wrote on the last page.

In spite of all the interruptions and obstacles, in spite of the disheartening experiences, struggles, and self-sacrifice, his great work lay finished before him after almost a quarter of a century of labor.

It could have been finished and performed in Zurich in 1859; Weimar was next thought of as the place of its christening; it was driven out of Munich by hostile force; and at last, by his own efforts, he had built a house for it on virgin soil. The work was finished on paper, but there was to be a repetition of many struggles and anxieties before it could be performed. No sooner was it finished than his publisher, Schott of Mayence, gave him no peace until he had written a whole series of "Introductions and Finale," so that single numbers could be used for concert purposes.

"Oh, Germany!" was his distressed cry.

### To Friedrich Feustel

(Bayreuth, December 16, 1874.)

*Dear good Friend!*

Still filled with gratitude for yesterday, I come to make another claim upon you to-day. I wished to inform you that Rth [1] 818 (for "Fliegender Holländer") have reached me to-day from Berlin; the entire sum I have kept for myself, for well-known outlay (for example, Kietz in Dresden for the marble bust, etc.), as well as for the calamities of the Christmas and New Year season. . . .

[1] Reichsthaler.

If for any reason you prefer another modus, and if you would rather have my baria go through your bureau, I beg of you to let me know your opinion.

Not until January shall I have any income worth speaking of, and then I shall incorporate this with our Conto corrent.

The chief impulse to " Forwards " in my finances I do not expect until April of this year, when, in addition to the presumably good receipts from the profitable quarterly payments, come those promised me by Schott.

So — one swims and wades! One hopes finally, however, to reach the shore — at least, when someone stands by you who has a resemblance to my friend Feustel! . . .

From his whole heart greets you

Your ever grateful and faithful

RICHARD WAGNER.

P.S.  The *Sgraffitto*[1] did cost something, after all!

---

[1] The fresco in *sgraffitto* work, which is placed over the entrance of Wahnfried, was executed by Robert Krause.

To Professor Carl Doeppler

(Bayreuth, December 17, 1874.)

*Esteemed Sir!*

I permit myself to inquire if you would be favourably inclined to undertake the designing of the costumes, as well as the superintendence of the execution of the same, for the projected Festival performance of my four-part Stage Festival Play, the "Ring of the Nibelung," in the summer of 1876.

For your preliminary information as to the character of your task, I am sending you a copy of the dramatic text as well as several brochures referring to the execution of the same. You will recognise at once that it is the difficulties which have arisen in connection with the matter which have determined me upon looking about for an unusually experienced and excellent artist in this particular province.

I believe I am justified in regarding the task as a fertile field and one which offers great possibilities for an inventive mind. For, to get at the gist of the matter, I require nothing less than a characteristic painting executed in single figures, which shall present with striking vivacity individual events from each and every episode of this far-distant culture epoch. You will soon find that the picture which has been accepted as the authoritative characterisation of the figures in the mediæval Nibelung Epic, according to the precedent set by Cornelius, Schnorr, and others, must here be left quite out of the question. On the other hand, if one has given attention of late to the characterisations from the specific Northern mythology, it will have become apparent how an effort was being made to avoid difficulty by using a modification of the classic antique. Intimations of the Roman writers, who came in touch with the Germanic peoples as to the costumes of these people, do not seem to have received the attention they merit.

According to my opinion, any artist who wished to appropriate the sketches I gave him, and make them his own, would find a unique field, not only for intelligent compilation, but for his inventive fancy as well; and I could wish for nothing more than that you, highly esteemed sir, should assume this task.

Begging you to let me know your inclination in the matter, I do myself the honour of sending you greetings of especial respect as

Your humble servant,

RICHARD WAGNER.

# PRELIMINARY REHEARSALS

## The Year 1875

### To Emil Heckel

(BAYREUTH, December 31, 1874.)

*My dear Friend!*

In order that I may close the old year with something agreeable, I reply at once to your dear, dear greeting just received!

You dear just men, and particularly our chief co-worker, Zeroni! Be heartily greeted from me and mine!

Health, good spirits, and humour — in short, everything which one calls the gifts of God and of nature — are good. Here and there enormous difficulties,[1] but always leading to something good.

Beautiful, very beautiful, was your dear visit,

---

[1] In the original, "Hangen und Würgen."

you two chief " just men "!  But another time
bring also the wives of the just men.

You will soon receive accurate information as
to the progress of our preparations!

Above all things, a wish for a good year from
Yours faithfully,

RICHARD WAGNER.


To EMIL HECKEL

(BAYREUTH, January 2, 1875.)

*Dear Friend!*

Once again: a good New Year!  But now
come the worries, namely, the definite decisions
as to casting certain *rôles* for my work.  As I
have quite a collection of interrogation points
before me in regard to Mannheim, I appeal to
you as a diplomat, hoping you will do better by
me than Count Arnim did by Bismarck.

1.  Herr Unger shall make the effort to learn
the *Loge* and in addition study the *Siegmund* for
an emergency.  This could be of advantage to
him in the future, in case he is present at all of

the rehearsals, even should he not sing it just yet in Bayreuth.

2. Herr Knapp I should like to have for *Fafner*, on account of many characteristics; friend Langer must see if this is possible with Knapp's voice (on account of the deep tones). If *not*, then he shall stick to *Donner*, with the study of *Gunther* as doublette — just in the same way as Unger with *Siegmund*.

3. Fräulein Auguste v. Müller: "*Grimmgerde*," one of the Valkyries: *Erda* and *First Norn* for emergency, *vide:* Unger — *Siegmund*.

4. Fräulein Johanna König — the bird's voice in " Siegfried," — the somewhat slight figure of the lady preventing my making further use of her. I should like to have used her for the first Rhine daughter, *Woglinde;* but for this I need, above all, routined, experienced, and courageous women, as they sing most of the time in a flying machine for which the Lehmann sisters (Lilli and Marie) have offered themselves. *But:* caution is also advised here: Fräulein König

may as well study the *Woglinde*, just as it would be advisable for Fräulein v. Müller to study the *Flosshilde*.

Friend Langer is to look after all the coaching — these are the temporary machinations; if I receive good news from you as to the willingness of the above-mentioned singers, official measures, distribution of the *rôles*, more exact arrangements will follow. Only I must be absolutely assured of the *unconditional* willingness of the participants in every way; this was a point emphasised in my suggestion.

Artistic sensitiveness, coveting of *rôles*, and any demands of this nature will necessitate a complete breach whenever I meet with such conditions.

Only by the voluntary good-will of *all participants* can that which I have in view be successfully accomplished.

I still need a *Sieglinde:*[1] that is a *calamity!*

---

[1] The greatest trouble Wagner encountered in the casting of his work was in finding a suitable *Sieglinde* and *Siegfried*.

She must be slender and competent.  Frau Jaide will not answer.  Have you thought of anyone? In case Knapp does not wish to sing *Fafner*, do you know of any suitable fellow for the *rôle?* However, he must be a deep, powerful bass.

A thousand cordial greetings from house to house, and to the distinguished just men!

Your little old

RICHARD WAGNER.

TO EMIL HECKEL

(BAYREUTH, January 28, 1875.)

Well, here is the desired (circular).  We shall be able to manage eight or ten marks a day for those without means; *therefore* — say to the singers that they can make this condition.

Great care will be taken that my company receives good and *cheap* accommodations.

Good evening, dear friend.

Yours,

RICHARD WAGNER.

(Clerk.)

Heckel had made an inquiry concerning the amount which was to be allowed the artists for their living expenses while in Bayreuth, and at the same time he requested that a copy of the circular to the artists be sent him.

He received the latter with the lines above written on the back of it.

This circular which Wagner drew up in January, 1875, and had distributed among the artists whom he had in view for his Festival performances, read as follows:

" In the course of the personal intercourse with you, which it has been my privilege to enjoy, you have learned of my wish to secure your co-operation in carrying into effect, under absolutely unique conditions, a three-fold performance of my four-part stage work entitled the " Ring of the Nibelung."

" I believe that the realisation of this idea, which, on the one hand, has depended upon the extraordinary support of the friends and patrons of my art, çan only be made possible by the cordial and vigorous consent of the distinguished artists whose co-operation has been solicited, as the support of my patrons should and must only be given to an undertaking in connection with which there is no thought of money-making speculation. You will therefore find yourselves (perhaps for the first time in your lives) called upon to devote your gifts solely and singly to the achievement of an ideal artistic purpose, namely, that of showing to the German public what the German is able to do with his art on his own native ground, and in this way be able to present to foreign countries, from whose artistic leavings we have lived chiefly up to this time, something which they are not capable of imitating."

Here follow the obligations and conditions upon which this invitation was to be accepted, and an accurate statement of the time and length of the rehearsals, with a request that the artists name the sum which would cover their expenses.

The letter closed with the following clause:

" I now await your favourable answer, in order to learn that I shall be able to count you among those who have bound themselves voluntarily into a confederation of the highest significance, and pledged themselves to carry into execution an artistic idea such as was never before projected."

## To Carl Brandt

(Not dated.)

*Dearest Colleague!*

When I got home, I found the letter which I at once send on to you. I believe we may trust this man, as the English in this particular point [1] are somewhat ahead of us.

Will you kindly write to the man whatever there is to be said? And also make closer inquiries as to his work?

---

[1] This refers to the Dragon in "Siegfried," which was eventually ordered from the man mentioned here for £500. It was transported in sections and caused the greatest anxiety in Bayreuth.

When all of the various detachments had finally arrived, Fricke, the ballet-master, was so disgusted that he cried: "Away to the attic with such a monster!"

With cordial greetings and many thanks for your last visit,

Yours,

RICHARD WAGNER.


To EMIL HECKEL

(BAYREUTH, February 6, 1875.)

*Dear Friend!*

To *you* therefore — as always — briefly and to the point!

Knapp bores me somewhat with the absurd-sounding clause in regard to certain particular deductions. Eilers and other excellent artists, as well as the poor Unger, accept the simple compensation — Eilers, in fact, only ninety thalers a month. Eilers sings two of the chief *rôles* for me, while I can only count on Knapp of a certainty for the *Donner*, and for the same *rôle* I could have Degele in Dresden for nothing. If Herr Knapp insists upon his fifteen marks (per day), I can only use him for the first week in July and the first week in August of this

year, and he can then earn money elsewhere in
the interim.

Honestly, this haggling annoys me! I will
write personally to Unger, Fräulein König, and
Fräulein von Müller. Otherwise everything is
going very well, and a great effort is being made
on every side to lighten the expenses for me.

Richter has just been here on his wedding
journey. On the 11th of this month we start
ourselves for Pesth and Vienna. Be in Vienna
evening of March 1st. (Nothing but " Götterdämmerung "!)

Cordial greetings from house to house!

Wholly and entirely yours,

RICHARD WAGNER.

Hans Richter came to Bayreuth, not only to
discuss the approaching concert in Pesth, where
he was at that time musical director, but to introduce his bride to Wagner.

As a wedding present, Wagner had sent him
the newly published score of the " Walküre "

Doctor Hans Richter

with some humourous dedicatory lines referring to the firm attitude taken by Richter during the "Rheingold" period in Munich.

"Gedenkt dass noch in fernen Tagen,
  Wie Richter und Wagner es einst mochten wagen,
  Eher Werk und Taktstock zu zerschlagen,
  Als die Welt mit schlechtem Aufführungen zu plagen."

## To Friedrich Feustel

(Vienna, February 27, 1875.)

*My dearest Friend!*

Your kind letter pleased and gratified me greatly. Accept my thanks for your so unusually considerate friendship.

I regret that you are still obliged to keep up such a "lively" correspondence with Schott, as I can only infer this to mean that you are meeting with difficulties.

. . . Here (Vienna) I at once met with great vexation. But now, thanks to my extraordinary efforts, everything is going well. But it will not be easy to bring the receipts up to the desired amount. The calamity here is so great at the present that my friends have not dared to ask the same high prices that they did three years ago; instead of twenty-five florins at that time, they could venture on only twenty, and so on in proportion, so that the highest gross receipts to be expected will be twelve thousand florins. Everywhere astonishment reigns that at a time of general stagnation, when many theatres have been obliged to close their doors on account of lack of an audience, the name of R. W. has been able to work such a miracle.

In Pesth it will not be very different, and I shall be obliged to renounce all idea of large receipts; however, I have resolved to equalise matters by repeating the concert in Vienna on March 4, namely, at lower prices, in order that the less-well-off public (who are pining for this) will be able to come.

It is to be assumed that this second concert will also be filled to overflowing, and that the receipts will prove satisfactory, as the expenses will be very little.

Within the next few days I shall suggest to the King, from obligatory considerations, a private performance of the same numbers in the Residenz Theatre. Whether he accepts this or not, I intend in any case to return by way of Munich in order to see and hear the artist pair Vogel.

My wife joins me in greetings and thanks!

I remain always

Your deeply grateful

RICHARD WAGNER.

TO EMIL HECKEL

(BAYREUTH, March 26, 1875.)

*Dear Friend Heckel!*

Many thanks! Much trouble and vexation — I gladly await Herr v. Reichenberg, but my time is short [1] which brings me to ask you to arrange the affairs with Herr Knapp. Since the conductors are behaving so badly, I have grown tired of the haggling and bargaining,

---

[1] In German, "Knapp."

and moreover Herr Knapp really interests me. Let him dispose of his time according to the order of the rehearsals. I need him only for the " Rheingold," and, provided he will sing one of the men in the " Götterdämmerung," the other numbers he can use for concert work, etc. Moreover, I should not care to make payments to the Mannheim Pension Fund during the time that he is lying here idle.

In regard to Unger I am rather uncertain just at present. You know that!

I am expecting news which will result in my seeing " Tristan " in Munich April 5th at the latest; if Frau Vogel fulfils my expectations and I am able to secure her for *Sieglinde*, this will undoubtedly depend upon my taking her husband also. I can give him no other *rôle* than that of *Loge*. For this reason I do not see at present what I could do with Unger, whom I know so little. He, however, has left an impression which decides me *in any case* to become better acquainted with him. He must therefore spend some time in my neighbourhood, purely for the *cause* and in order to profit by my instructions. I cannot, however, make any compensation to him for his sojourn here.

Now do see what is to be done! In the event that Frau Vogel definitely displeases me, Unger would then serve for *Loge*.

I have passed through much lately and am also not at all well.

But in the end everything must succeed.

Cordial greetings from

Your faithful

RICHARD WAGNER.

To CARL BRANDT

(BAYREUTH, April 6, 1875.)

*Dear Herr Brandt!*

You can see what kind of people I have to do with in Darmstadt! Still no word has been received from the Kapellmeister there!!! I fear I shall be obliged to renounce all claim on the Darmstadt Orchestra. And now another thing which makes my heart heavy!

I was at the theatre again to-day, and must confess that, unless I wish to perjure myself shamefully, the architect has built my orchestra pit *absolutely incorrect.*

I cannot accommodate my musicians in *this* space. It is quite impossible! *Nothing* remains to be done but to remove two rows of seats from the auditorium (which is of no concern) and to take away the dividing wall and put it farther back.

I will point this out to Runckwitz to-morrow (will you have the kindness, at the same time, to put yourself into communication with Mr. — Henry VIII.[1]) in Leipzig.

I remember to have heard you say, on this point, earlier, that there would be no fundamental difficulties in the way of removing the wall.

It is a matter of absolute indifference to me, in the plan as a whole, if a hundred listeners more or less are accommodated. The thing is to present a perfect performance in every re-

[1] Brückwald — his name just occurs to me!

spect — the rest is a matter of indifference.  But
your Darmstadt musicians!  And no one upon
whom I can rely but the poor " machinist," whom
I greet most cordially as his

Faithful

Richard Wagner.


To Friedrich Feustel

(Berlin, April 16, 1875.)

*Dearest Friend!*

Best thanks for your letter which I found
awaiting me here, and which made me feel at
home, although it contained no very encouraging news. . . .

My trip, upon which I started eight days ago,
has been so far only a chase after singers.  I
have not been entirely unlucky in this respect,
and I also made the very delightful acquaintance
of the Braunschweig impresario, which I almost
dare to hope will lead to the Duke becoming a
patron.  Everything here is said to be going
well.  I have resolved to follow up to the very

last point all the resources which Berlin offers me. Unfortunately this all costs a great deal of money, which often seems to be an unnecessary expenditure. . . .

May we recommend our children and our house to the kind care of you and yours, and for this all of you are most heartily greeted by me and my wife.

Always yours gratefully and faithfully,

RICHARD WAGNER.

TO FRIEDRICH FEUSTEL

(BAYREUTH, May 2, 1875.)

*My dearest Friend!*

How right you were to insist, above all, that the artistic details in the execution of my undertaking should be the chief consideration, and that our slender and painfully accrued funds should not be wasted upon the exterior of our theatre! The very justifiable warning, which was moreover accompanied by a side glance at our treasury, immediately decided me to limit the excavations to such as are absolutely indispensable for the immediate environment of the theatre.

In any case I wish to return to the city the entire piece of ground reaching from the theatre terrace to the extreme front entrance, with the serious suggestion that this large piece of ground be used entirely according to the wisdom of the City Council. If needs be, the *chaussée* already built can be used profitably as a street.

I shall content myself, then, with the still very considerable space which now forms a plateau surrounding the theatre; the entrance and exit can take place by way of the *chaussée* leading to Burgerreuth. I found yesterday, in a conversation with Herr Runckwitz, that this could easily be accomplished.

The young building master told me also that about five thousand florins have already been expended on the excavations; I wish now that the contracts (with especial consideration for certain contractors) be annulled, and then I would set aside about two thousand to three thousand florins for the levelling of the plateau, so that the entire work of excavation would cost, for the present at least, only eight thousand florins.

For, in the first place, I have to keep in mind the rehearsals this summer. If the next concert in Vienna succeeds according to my expectations, then I may well claim the credit of having created the necessary financial basis for these rehearsals. It shall now be my chief concern to hold this intact for these rehearsals; on the other hand, the fact that the city of Bayreuth will have to transform a large piece of ground into a park for the Sunday promenades of its citizens, cannot be laid to my ambition.

In the same way I shall refrain from having anything further to do with the agitation concerning the hotel question. In response to my very first inquiry in regard to the accommodation of strangers, I received the assurance of the city of Bayreuth, through my representative, that this question would be satisfactorily solved, and it was only upon receiving *this* promise that I decided upon Bayreuth as the home of my Festival Play.

I now rely upon the sense of honour of my new fellow citizens, and in the future shall only keep in view the purely artistic success of my undertaking.

In any case I shall present my work to the German public in three successive performances; as to whether out of this a permanent institution will be formed or not for the benefit of the city of Bayreuth will depend largely upon what Bayreuth does in the matter.

I hope, dearest friend, that you agree with me in my view of the situation, as well as in my decisions concerning the same, and in this assumption I beg of you to suggest a way by which my appeal to the city to take back part of the ground given me may best be accomplished, as well as the solution of the question concerning the annulling of the contracts for the excavations.

I hope I shall see you before my departure, which, however, takes place to-morrow after-noon. In the meantime I greet you as ever.

Your deeply grateful

RICHARD WAGNER.

(Saturday, May 2, 1875.)

The night in which my good Russ suddenly died.

The material results of the two Berlin concerts amounted to only six thousand thalers; the expenses were borne by the Berlin Wagner Society, which demanded in return six Patrons' Certificates.

Wagner felt himself under obligations to use this small sum, which was so incommensurate with the effort expended in obtaining it, for the approaching rehearsals, and not devote it to the grounds around the theatre.

The postscript is full of significance, as the dog Russ had been Wagner's faithful companion for nine years; he had belonged to the happy

Triebschen days and had come with the family to Bayreuth. At the time of the erection of Villa Wahnfried, Wagner had his vault built in the garden back of the house and covered it with a plain granite slab. At the foot of this the faithful Russ was buried, and on a small stone tablet the inscription is still to be read: " Here rests and watches Wagner's Russ."

## To Emil Heckel

(BAYREUTH, May 27, 1875.)

Best thanks to all

The Just Men and their Wives!

My good wife delighted me with a splendid garden *fête* on my birthday!

But: —

*Business!* —

Unger still has n't put in his appearance, although I have twice telegraphed him that I had something important in view for him. I fear I shall be obliged to give him up at the very start. . . .

Pardon me! But your little questions about

this or that, as to whether or not anyone can be admitted to the rehearsals? . . . etc. often demand answers which are not so easy to give, — for I am much more worried than you seem to think.

This year's *Preparatory Studies, not rehearsals*, are to be devoted entirely to the matter in hand and not to an audience; from the 1st to the 15th of August, however, there will be orchestra rehearsals for placing, seating, sound, and first reading of the score.

Whoever happens to be there and conducts himself modestly will eventually have an opportunity of hearing something, but no special *permissions* for this will be given out.

What difficulties there still are ahead of me!

May all the just men realise this and not be continually congratulating me beforehand on my " successes."

Many cordial greetings.

Yours,

RICHARD WAGNER.

The rehearsals were imminent, and it was to get these under way that Wagner had come back to Bayreuth. During his long absence the work had accumulated; new singers were to be tried, *rôles* were to be distributed, and in the eleventh hour he was still without an interpreter for his *Siegfried*.

Only a Schnorr, the creator of *Tristan*, seemed adequate for this second heroic *rôle*, but this great singer had died suddenly in 1865, and his loss Wagner mourned afresh when it came to casting the important *rôle* of *Siegfried*. Various singers had been tested but had been found wanting, and Georg Unger seemed to be the only one who could come under serious consideration.

This choice was due not so much to Unger's unusual vocal gifts as to his personal appearance and great stature, which fitted him admirably for the joyous youthful hero, *Siegfried*.

The conditions upon which he was accepted at Bayreuth were that he should leave the stage for a year and devote himself exclusively to the preparation of the *rôle*, and in addition devote himself to serious voice work with Professor Julius Hey in Munich.

Wagner himself studied the *rôle* with him word by word, note by note, and wrought a marvellous transformation in Unger both as an actor and an artist. Hey, in his " Reminiscences," writes that:

" The sixty-two-year-old Wagner not only made clear to Unger every passage of the ' Siegfried ' score, in regard to meaning, mood, vocal technic, and plasticity in the treatment of the text, but also endeavoured to influence his entire character, so as to bring Unger into closer harmony with that of the ' hero without fear.' "

Wagner, according to the testimony of his artists, had a marvellous gift of vitalizing the music, and as a singer without a voice he made the dramatic situation so vivid as to create an indelible impression upon all present. Hey relates a little anecdote from the " Siegfried " rehearsal, where at the point where *Mime* utters his second distressed cry of "Fafner!" Wagner's voice broke on the high A, producing an irresistibly comical effect. He laughed immoderately, as did everyone else, and cried: "Where shall I hide myself! There is no anvil here!"

To quote Hey further: "How did this voice, which in reality was no voice at all, succeed in producing such moving tone nuances, so as to present in the clearest manner every varying phase of emotion! And in addition a dramatic declamation which penetrated to the very bottom of the listener's soul!"

### To Emil Heckel

(Bayreuth, June 6, 1876.)

*Dear Friend!*

I beg of you to make inquiries about Brahms' present residence and have this letter sent to him.

Everything is going on fairly well! More later!

Yours faithfully,

Richard Wagner.

In order to understand this reference to Brahms, it is necessary to go back almost a decade and a half in the life of Wagner, to the period when he returned from his Parisian exile. He went to Vienna, where there seemed to be a somewhat vague prospect for a performance of his " Tristan," which, however, eventually took place in Munich in 1865. The friends who stood nearest to him at this time were Peter Cornelius and Carl Tausig, the former of whom, out of genuine enthusiasm for the Master and his music, had offered to copy the score of the Parisian arrangement of the " Tannhäuser," as the original one was much the worse for wear.

When this labour of love was finished, the Cornelius copy (with German text) was given to Wagner, and the original manuscript (in French) Cornelius coolly kept for himself, although nothing was further from Wagner's intentions than to make him a present of it. Later this original manuscript, at that time unpublished, in some mysterious way came into the possession of Carl

Tausig, who took the further liberty of giving it to none other than Johannes Brahms, a musician considered by the Wagnerian party to be the arch enemy of the music being made by the Master of Bayreuth.

In August, 1865, Wagner made an attempt to regain possession of the original manuscript and demanded that Cornelius should write to Brahms. This he did, but the letter remained unanswered. He also wrote to Tausig, saying:

"That is a stupid affair with Brahms! You are supposed to have given him that scene from 'Tannhäuser'!"

Wagner's wife, at that time the wife of Hans von Bülow, also wrote to Brahms, but in vain.

The only intimation he gave of having received these various requests is found in a few lines to Cornelius saying that he did "not wish to return the manuscript *given* him." Years went by, and finally Wagner was obliged to take the matter in hand, as he needed the manu-

script for the new edition of the " Tannhäuser "
scene.

In order to make sure that the letter containing a personal request should reach Brahms, he
sent it in care of Heckel.

The request read: " I am told that you claim
this manuscript on the ground that it was given
to you by Peter Cornelius, but I am not able
to credit this statement, as Cornelius, to whom
I lent but by no means gave this manuscript,
could not possibly have passed it on to a third
person, and he solemnly assures me that he did
not do so.   It is probably unnecessary to re-
mind you of these facts, and assume that no
further explanation will be necessary in order
to induce you to return the manuscript, which
for you could have only the value of a curiosity,
but which to my son would be a highly valued
souvenir."   Still Brahms adhered to the standpoint that possession is nine points of the law,
and it was not until Frau Wagner had written
that he consented to an exchange, by the terms of

which he was to have a copy of the " Meistersinger " score, and a page of some original Wagner manuscript, but in the end had to content
himself with an edition *de luxe* of the " Rheingold " score.   This is the Brahms episode as it
is recorded by C. F. Glasenapp.

### To Friedrich Feustel

(Bayreuth, June 9, 1875.)

*Dearest Friend!*

There seems to be no end of my demands upon
you for payments of various sorts, without my
having been able to deposit with your treasurer
fresh supplies for myself.   This I hope to be
able to do within the next few days. . . .

I shall try to keep my time free for the next
meeting of our " circle," and beg of you to inform the gentlemen this evening that I hope to
beg their pardon in sackcloth and ashes next
Thursday.

*Ach, Gott!* if friends would just drop in any
evening!   The devil is to pay here at eight

o'clock; there is always beer and also cigars; you could seat yourselves in the garden before the music-room and we would make music for you.  But — ?!

Cordial greetings from

Your ever grateful

RICHARD WAGNER.

To EMIL HECKEL

(BAYREUTH, June 25, 1875.)

How now! Friend Heckel! Do you change your opinion so easily? Not long ago you defended Unger — now you believe in Jager? — Well, I have already begun with Unger, and have taken a great deal of trouble in overcoming his Saxon vocalisation, which made his voice completely unrecognisable, until now I hope to be able to get along with him better than any tenor I know. I shall keep him here all the time; he was apparently lost, but he is a person not without energy. Jager is excellent, but —

The entertainment question is now entering a new phase: we shall be obliged to manage without building any new hotels.

Cordial greetings from

Your faithful composer,

RICHARD WAGNER.


TO CARL BRANDT

(Visiting card, not dated.)
(At the theatre.)

*To Herr Carl Brandt.*

Professor Doeppler is here with beautiful designs.  Do come, if not at once to supper, at least as soon as possible.

R. W.


The first musical sounds which were heard in the new Festival Theatre were on June 24, 1875.

The entire artist *personnel*, as well as many invited guests, had assembled to inspect the new scenery for " Rheingold " and " Die Walküre." When Wagner had satisfied himself that all was in order, he clasped his hands and cried:

" Now, children, go on the stage and let us hear something! "

The women climbed over the frail planks bridging the orchestral pits and gave with irresistible effect the first scene from the " Rheingold," with Alberick's sinister voice sounding from some invisible corner.

The three singers who were to open the " Ring " with the beautiful *terzet* of the Rhine maidens were Lilli Lehmann, her sister Marie, and Fräulein Lammert.

To present this scene with proper realism was one of the most difficult problems with which the stage machinists were confronted.

Not only had the singers to make the movements which would correspond with the music and suggest their watery home, but these same movements must be executed by the cages in which they were fastened.

One man was needed to steer the Undines, another to see that they were raised, lowered, or shifted at the proper time, and such musicians as Anton Seidl, Felix Mottl, and Franz Fischer, each one provided with a carefully marked score, sat in the cages to give the signal for the various movements to the machinists.

Wagner was in a terrible state of anxiety over this scene, but was comforted after seeing the detailed plan which Richard Fricke, his ballet-master, had worked out for its satisfactory execution.

Fricke compared the three young directors with their scores to dancers executing a *pas de trois*, and gave frank expression to his doubts concerning the singers: " It is not clear to me how the singers will have the courage to lie in such a machine — and, moreover, to sing. Not alone on account of the difficulty of singing in a half-upright position, but they will not be able to produce a tone out of sheer fright. I am very curious to see how it will turn out."

Three of the men belonging to the band of *Nibelungs* were first put into the cages as *figurantes*, and then the day came when the three

Rhine maidens were to perform their task for the first time. As soon as Lilli Lehmann caught sight of the cages, she cried: "No, no one could expect me to do such a thing; I shall not do it under any circumstances. I am just out of a sick-bed, and am already as dizzy as I can be."

Fricke used his powers of persuasion to better purpose with Marie, who with shrieks and cries was strapped into her cage and the "swimming" lesson began. Upon her solemn assurance that "it was not as bad as it looked," Lilli Lehmann and Fräulein Lammert let themselves be persuaded, and were soon swimming about in the bravest possible manner. Wagner was beside himself with joy, and embraces and kisses were the immediate reward of his courageous Rhine maidens.

On the 1st of August, 1875, the orchestral and ensemble rehearsals began.

It was then that the effect of the invisible orchestra was tested. Wagner assigned his musicians their place in the "mystic abyss," according to the arrangement which to-day is so convincing. The strings were placed under the upper sounding-board, the harps and woodwinds in the uncovered space, in order that their delicate quality might assert itself, and the brasses and instruments of percussion were relegated to a position under the stage projection, in order that the aggressiveness of their tone might be modified. The results justified in the highest degree the expectations of Wagner and the assembled listeners. The volume of sound surprised by its ideal tonal beauty; everything material seemed to have been fully eliminated, and every figuration, even in the middle voices, came out with startling distinctness. The most painstaking effort was expended upon every detail of the performance.

How could it be otherwise when a conductor with the ardour of Hans Richter was at the helm, and when the violinist, August Wilhelmj, performed the functions of concert-master; when each musician was filled with ardent enthusiasm, and when encompassing the whole was Wagner's spirit, arranging, supervising, inspiring, and encouraging! For every detail he found a remedy, which was often the result of momentary inspiration, and much, which neither the printed text nor the carefully marked score revealed, suggested itself only at the moment of actual contact of the work with the stage.

A small table furnished with a petroleum lamp and a box which served as a support for the score was placed for Wagner on the stage, and from this vantage-point he kept watch over the conductor and the progress of events on the stage.

A picture of Wagner as he appeared at these rehearsals has been preserved for us by the genius of Adolph von Menzel, the great German historical painter.

Wagner's idea in these rehearsals was not to proceed from the single point to the whole, but just the reverse. First the whole, and then the working out of details, so that as a result of this method something relatively perfect was accomplished, and the rehearsals, so far as orchestral and voice parts were concerned, differed but little from the eventual public performances.

Everyone who was permitted to take part in these rehearsals in any capacity whatever had the feeling that here a new epoch of musical history was being ushered in.

Among the invited guests was Franz Liszt, who gave expression to this same thought in a letter written at that time: "I recently heard twenty rehearsals of that wonderful work 'The Nibelung's Ring.' It towers over and dominates our art epoch as does Mont Blanc the other mountain peaks."

Three years earlier, Wilhelmj's official appointment to his responsible post was made by Wagner in the following letter:

(BAYREUTH, June 3, 1872.)

*My dear Herr Wilhelmj!*

Upon my largest sheet of writing paper, I confirm your appointment as

*Concert-Master of the Orchestra*

for the performance of the

" Ring of the Nibelung "

in

*Bayreuth.*

As I see that your delightful offer to stand by me in the capacity of concert-master was not made jestingly, it is only fitting that I should also take the matter very seriously, as you will see from the above.

With the greatest seriousness, my friend, let us from to-day pledge ourselves to think solicitously of the formation of our orchestra, above all, of an orchestra free from the traditional evil habits; to exchange opinions on the subject, and at all times to take such steps as will insure an organisation of great excellence.

You undoubtedly wish and desire this as much as I do; this I recognised in you, who at such an early age have become so celebrated a master of your instrument.

Let us then, from now on, be united in this

extraordinary work, and permit me, in addition to all the other arrangements which will be made to your satisfaction, to proclaim you as my valued Master of Musicians, as which you will participate in all the success which will not be denied our work. With the most cordial greetings from me and my wife, I remain

Yours faithfully,

RICHARD WAGNER.

To CARL BRANDT

(BAYREUTH, September 21, 1875.)

*Dear and valued Friend!*

We have got into a terrible state of procrastination, and I turn to you, as my sole real confidant and sympathetic associate in the work, to enjoin upon you to exert all of your strength to change matters.

What help would it be to me to insist upon Brückner's coming over to Bayreuth if you were not here at the same time? Brückwald pretends to be without help in executing his models, but promises to be ready in time.

Now *you* arrange a time for a general meeting; this must take place in October, because I am obliged to be at Vienna during November and half of December. Therefore, after consulting with the others, you decide this matter, and I shall support you by especial exhortations to the parties concerned. So let it be! And accept cordial greetings from

Your very faithful

RICHARD WAGNER.

TO FRIEDRICH FEUSTEL

(VIENNA, November 4, 1875.)

*Dearest Friend!*

I have taken cold and am exhausted and kept back by the bad accommodations in the hotel decided upon beforehand. Since yesterday, however, I am well taken care of in Hotel Imperial, and expect to continue the rehearsals to-morrow.

For to-day only the information, as briefly as possible, that it is settled that the royal residence in Bayreuth shall be left for the royal guests;

if the Emperor should come, the King of Bavaria would give up his own suite; as for the rest, nothing but the most distressing complaints and disclosures about — the well-known conditions.

This is what I wanted to write you. Now remain faithful to me, as I shall always remain grateful to you.

Cordially yours,

RICHARD WAGNER.

## To EMIL HECKEL

(VIENNA, November 11, 1875.)

*Allervorzüglichster Patronenlader!* [1]

Otherwise it is going so-so! — A cantor, Fischer, in Zwickau, has recently collected six and three-quarter Patrons' Certificates, sent six thousand marks, with the inquiry if this sum would entitle him to a free seat (!!!). "Tannhäuser" here the 21st of this month (!!) — I have none of the rehearsal plans with me; have

---

[1] No English equivalent can be found for this inscription, as the expression *Patronenlader* is a play on words referring to Heckel's efforts in regard to the Society of Patrons.

one sent you from Feustel or Fischer ("Nibe-lung Kanzelei").

Many cordial greetings from your harassed

RICHARD WAGNER.

### To FRIEDRICH FEUSTEL

(VIENNA, November 14, 1875.)

. . . Does our great cause seem to be moving forward without interruption? Yesterday a Prince ——ski made inquiries concerning Patrons' Certificates; referred him to you.

Heckel announces four items, etc. I suffer here from great weariness and take but little pleasure in the matter. In the forenoon, very taxing rehearsals, when I am obliged to show these people how to do everything; after this, complete change of clothing, rest in bed; towards evening, a little exercise (without Angermann).[1]

---

[1] Kietz, the Dresden sculptor, has given a picture of this favourite resort of Wagner and his disciples in his reminiscences:

"What life there is here! It is impossible to recognise the Bayreuth of 1873. The quiet streets of the little ducal residence are full of people. At Angermann's, in the long narrow room which the artists have christened 'The Catacombs,' there are the most hilarious proceedings. After the rehearsals everyone goes to the 'Catacombs.'"

In the evening, the theatre (very bad!) or some tiresome entertainment.

The sole consolation is that it is progressing, and I hope to be at home again by the middle of December at the latest.

The children are already looking forward to the day of our departure.  A thousand greetings, dearest friend, and at least five hundred for the good Gross.[1]

Ever in faithful gratitude,

Yours devotedly,

RICHARD WAGNER.

[1] The right-hand man of Feustel during the troublesome Bayreuth days was his son-in-law, Adolph Gross, who from the very beginning was initiated with every detail connected with the enterprise, and his knowledge of persons and things was so extensive and so accurate that he was a living archive of Bayreuth.

He was destined to be the future "Bismarck of Bayreuth" and to despatch misunderstandings, confusion, and threatened dangers with statesmanlike ability.

# THE FIRST BAYREUTH FESTIVAL

## 1876

### To Carl Brandt

(Bayreuth, January 3, 1876.)

*My dear Friend!*

I regret exceedingly to have heard nothing of you for so long! No other cause of anxiety leads me to write to you than this — because it is always so comforting for me to receive a sign of life from you. We are, of a truth, the only two who have understood each other from the beginning as to the execution of the work, and the most beautiful experience so far was the reception on your finished stage. Why have you not thought even once of me of late?

There are many reasons which excuse my silence!

I have not had an easy time since the close of our rehearsals. Surrounded by deceivers, contract breakers, and scoundrels of all sorts, it has been long since I have drawn a free breath.

I have really nothing to say to you at present about business. Difficulties of all sorts, and yet a firm will and confidence!

Frau Jaide has written me a very nice letter. She is evidently the biggest artistic talent and the most sensible artist in our *ensemble*. I was right in estimating her highly from the very start. It is possible that, without being given one of the larger *rôles*, she will serve me best by undertaking two episodes, both of which require as conspicuous an artist as do the largest *rôles*.

Without such an artist it would be impossible to give these episodes with the strong effect necessary, and in which lie the strength and distinction of our performances as a whole.

Remember me to this great artist and promise her a speedy token of my esteem!

And now hearty greetings to son, mother,

daughter, and, above all, to your wife.    The same from my wife, the much-tormented one!

Both of us look forward to receiving good news from you.

Cordially,

Your faithful colleague,

RICHARD WAGNER.


To EMIL HECKEL

(BAYREUTH, February 4, 1876.)

*Dearest, best Friend!*

In answer to the question "How are all of you?" there is much that could be said! The world, and particularly Germania, is becoming more and more odious to me!

Our cares are great, and, on the whole, the project of allowing our performances to take place this year seems foolhardy. The number of our Patrons' Certificates reaches only four hundred and ninety; while, according to the latest calculations, thirteen hundred are necessary in order to come out even.

A sketch by Adolph Menzel of Wagner at Bayreuth

The undertaking as originally planned is therefore fully shipwrecked. Now we must take the risk of seeing what curiosity will eventually do for our cause. Even Feustel believes that we may make this venture; but we anticipate a lack of funds in June, etc., when the musicians and singers arrive and will wish to draw their money. I solicited a loan of thirty thousand thalers from the Emperor. When I go to Berlin in May to look after "Tristan," — in which I have no great faith, — I shall see what can be done. For the rest, we must put a good face on the matter here. Everything will be ready (on *credit!*); the artistic details of the performance will be carried out to a point of the highest perfection. Brandt — as ever, excellent — my chief support.

Aside from Scaria,[1] I have come across no re-

<hr />

[1] Emil Scaria was a Vienna singer, whom Wagner hoped to secure for the *role* of *Hager*, but his demands seemed so excessive that he was obliged to relinquish the idea, and the first Bayreuth Festival took place without the desired co-operation of Scaria. Wagner who recognised this artist's talent and capacity for the *role*, wrote to him: "If any rich man or monarch were backing me, as you erroneously seem to suppose, I should not hesitate to comply with your demands secretly!" Fortunately Scaria was a

luctance among the singers; everyone seems to stick to the cause with fine courage. I shall know how to help myself even if Scaria does not mend his ways at the last moment; however, I have not entirely given him up yet. Otherwise there is nothing new. Cordial greetings to your wife and friends from me and mine. If you could practise a little sorcery, it would be most welcome to me.

But I remain always

Yours most faithfully,

RICHARD WAGNER.


Wagner had returned to his former scheme of making a direct appeal to the German Emperor, as he had learned that a certain sum for the advancement of national interests had been placed at this monarch's disposal, to be used as he deemed best.

conspicuous exception, as the other artists gave themselves heart and soul to the undertaking, and only demanded sufficient compensation to make it possible for them to devote all of their time to the rehearsals.

Wagner writes that he had been assured that the Emperor had agreed to this request and had recommended it to the chancellorship, but the finance minister Delbrück had dissuaded the Emperor from his purpose.

From his private funds the Emperor took twenty-five Patrons' Certificates, but the small sum was but a fraction of the million marks necessary to establish for all time a model theatre — to make of Bayreuth, in fact, a high school of German art.

It was only when King Ludwig again came to the rescue with a loan of two hundred thousand marks that Wagner decided to adhere to his plan of having the Festival in 1876.

In addition to these anxieties about his great enterprise, he was weighed down with cares of a private nature.  He had built and furnished Villa Wahnfried, which had become a rendezvous for the Bayreuth *personnel* and guests, and this broad hospitality demanded unceasing expenditure.

To Emil Heckel

(BAYREUTH, April 8, 1876.)

*Dearest Friend!*

Within the next few days an announcement will be made in regard to the free places, which will undoubtedly prove highly satisfactory to you!

Cordial greetings,

Yours,

RICHARD WAGNER.

OPEN LETTER TO BURGOMASTER MUNCKER

(BAYREUTH, June 4, 1876.)

*Highly esteemed Herr Burgomaster!*

A short time ago the local " Tageblatt " contained a friendly welcome to the artists who are now arriving to take part in the approaching Festival Play, and I take it for granted that this editorial expression voiced the sentiments of the citizens of Bayreuth. I now feel impelled, in the name of the artists as well as in my own position as citizen of the town which has bestowed upon you the honourable position of its first magistrate, to express to you my gratitude for the unusual solicitude which you especially, Herr Burgomaster, have given to the reception and entertainment of my guests.

It is a task which has required genuine self-sacrifice on your part.

Nor can I make any allusion to this feature of your very effective co-operation without expressing my appreciation of the active and untiring support which you, in conjunction with the entire local administrative body of Bayreuth, have devoted for years to the advancement of this part of our enterprise.

It is only here upon the spot, after close scrutiny of the effective participation of the city authorities, that all those who until now had not been able to understand why a larger and healthier city was not chosen for the execution of my plans were obliged to confirm the wisdom of my choice. In no other place would

I have been assured of such a degree of self-sacrificing support on the part of the Civic Council, and it was this which prepossessed me so strongly upon my first acquaintance with the leading local authorities.

Even though I am obliged to reserve for the more fitting moment of our final great success an adequate expression of my gratitude for the unusually effective, yes, unique, sympathy offered by the Administrative Council, composed of yourself and your highly esteemed friends, to the unusually difficult execution of my plans, I hold it, nevertheless, to be my duty to-day to express my appreciation of the work of the civic administration of Bayreuth, as I have been surprised to see the zeal of the same administration exposed to suspicion in announcements made public within the last few days. Our local affairs have such a wide-reaching interest that these announcements could easily lead to incredibly false constructions and misunderstandings.

In the consciousness of having written in this

letter quite in accordance with the sentiments of our recently welcomed artistic guests, I greet you also, in the name of my artistic colleagues, esteemed Herr Burgomaster, and remain with unceasing gratitude and the highest respect,

Yours very faithfully,

RICHARD WAGNER.

TO BURGOMASTER THEODOR MUNCKER

(BAYREUTH, July 23, 1876.)

*Highly esteemed Friend!*

I have only just seen the announcement of the Executive Council, according to which my wish to try the acoustics of the hall next Tuesday by filling it, is to be met by offering the seats for sale.

I cannot possibly allow this, as we are obliged to rehearse very seriously that day (with a quite new singer, Herr Siehr), and while I could well afford to allow my local acquaintances and friends to be present, I could never extend this permission to those who paid for admission, as

amongst them would assuredly be found extremely critical and questionable elements.

I beg of you to induce our esteemed friends
of the Executive Council to retract this announcement, as otherwise I should find myself compelled
to change the rehearsal.

With the deepest respect,

Yours,

RICHARD WAGNER.

Wagner had intended that this acoustic trial
should be done by filling the house with soldiers
from the Bayreuth barracks.

To BURGOMASTER THEODOR MUNCKER

(BAYREUTH, July 23, 1876.)

*Most esteemed Herr Burgomaster!*

It was hinted to me this evening by our friend
Gross that our highly esteemed Herr Feustel
regards the countermanding of the attendance on
Tuesday " for pay " as an insult to himself, and

accordingly would withdraw his so very valuable assistance from our Executive Council.

In the face of this genuine calamity I resolved to let things take the course wished by Herr Feustel; after further consideration of the matter, I must, however, declare that I, for my part, will not be present at the rehearsal, and that I intend to leave the singers to themselves; may the consequences not prove injurious!

With respectful greetings,

Yours faithfully,

RICHARD WAGNER.

Inscription under a photograph of himself given to Emil Heckel immediately after the close of the first Festival.

O Freund Heckel
Es war doch gut!

RICHARD WAGNER.

(BAYREUTH, 1876.)

In an address to his *personnel* at the close of the rehearsal in 1875, Wagner said: " The first troubles have been overcome. Within a short time we must bring to perfection a genuine heroic deed. If we perform it in such a manner as I now distinctly see that we shall do, then we may well say with justice — we have done a great deed!"

And now the time had come to present this "great deed" to a half-confident, half-cynical, but wholly expectant art world.

On June 3 active preparations were resumed for the "Ring of the Nibelung." For six weeks these rehearsals continued; first the instrumental groups and vocalists were taken separately, next came the single acts, to each of which an entire day was devoted, and finally the complete drama was gone over.

The King of Bavaria had announced his intention of being present at the general rehearsal, which commenced on August 6; the house was absolutely empty with the exception of the solitary figure in the royal box, and a few persons closely associated with the work, who had been

permitted to take their places in the front rows
or had been smuggled into the gallery.

The presence of the royal patron served as a
spur to the artists and musicians, and the rehearsal varied in no detail from the regular
performance.

As was anticipated, however, the acoustics
were not satisfactory, and Wagner succeeded in
persuading his royal friend to allow the house
to be filled for the next performance.

An announcement was made that the holders
of Patrons' Certificates could obtain tickets for
the " Walküre " rehearsals, but as these alone
would not fill the house it was necessary to distribute the remainder of the tickets with the
greatest tact and discretion.

First to be considered were the Bayreuth hosts,
but many who had no claim for admittance succeeded in securing tickets, and the auditorium
presented an entirely different physiognomy from
the preceding day.

After the first act Wagner left the royal box

and appeared upon the stage, but was so moved that he could scarcely find words in which to thank his artists. He next visited the orchestral pit, and when the audience heard his voice, as he praised his musicians, a mighty cry of "Bravo for the Master!" went up from the auditorium.

At the close of the rehearsal cycle King Ludwig returned to Munich, but immediately sent a telegram from his castle of Hohenschwangan, thanking Wagner for the indelible impression which the work had made upon him, and announcing his intention of returning for the third regular cycle.

Three days later the theatre was filled with an eager and curious international crowd, among them many royal personages, at their head the venerable Emperor William I, and on August 13, 1876, all that Wagner had worked and wrought during the last quarter of a century took concrete form and became the *First Bayreuth Festival!*

The decisive moment had come when his artists had to be left to stand or fall alone. Everywhere in the wings and the *garderobe* he had posted his farewell exhortation:

"Last request to my faithful artists!
Distinctness!
The big notes will take care of themselves; the little notes and their text are the chief thing. Never say anything to the public, but always to each other; in monologues look either up or down, but never directly in front of you. Last wish: Be good to me, you dear children!"

For the orchestra, which he knew would be well taken care of by Hans Richter, the admonition was more concise:

"No preluding! Piano, pianissimo, and then all will be well!"

And now it remained to be proven whether or not the intellect and will of a single man would be able to lead, not only his artists, but the public as well, out of the old operatic grooves into the music of the future.

With the exception of a few technical details, the " Rheingold " was a perfect performance, but these trifling mishaps quite spoiled the evening for Wagner, who sat in his room back of the scenes abusing all the participants, and neither could he be induced to show himself on the stage, nor would he allow his artists to appear.

At the close of the " Götterdämmerung " the entire house rose with thundering bravos for the creator of this new art work.

Wagner's reply was full of significance. " We owe this to your favour, and the tireless energy of my artists. What I have to say to you can be expressed in an axiom! You have now seen what we can do; it remains with you to make it possible. And if it is your work, then we shall have an art."

This is the axiom which sounds through the centuries from the lips of every reformer of historical significance.

" Here I stand, I can do nothing else! "

The inadequacies which the entire performance displayed were clearer to Wagner than to anyone else.

The " style " which he hoped to form was not yet fully established; to whatever degree this work overtopped its epoch, it was still far from perfection and the ideal he had in mind.

Wagner's consolation was in the difficult hope entertained of being able to repeat the Festival the following year. " Next year it will all be different." No prophetic vision disclosed to him that it would be six years before the doors of the Festival Theatre would again be opened to present to the world the stage-consecrating play of " Parsifal "!

At the close of the Festival Wagner made an address, in the course of which he said:

" The Festival is now at an end, and I do not know whether or not it will occur again! I have called this work with its years of preparation a Festival Play — with what right, I cannot say, as historic annals record no feast day at this season of the year. It was designed with confidence in the German spirit and completed to the glory of its exalted patron, His Majesty the King of Bavaria, who has been not only its patron and promoter, but also a co-creator of the work."

## To Friedrich Feustel

*Dearest Friend!*     (Verona, September 18, 1876.)

Many thanks for all the solicitude expended upon me! I received everything, letter of credit, parcel 1, and to-day letters.

Unfortunately I spent yesterday in bed, and had so high a fever in the night that I am obliged to recover somewhat to-day, in order to go on to Venice to-morrow (Hotel Europa). The "Mistress of Risby" pleased me very much, and I beg for the continuation of the story. Of other newspapers such only as you consider important, but, on the other hand, send the two Leipzig music journals as regularly as possible. The good cousin Gross will look after my dogs once in a while.

Now I must take a thorough rest among the diversions offered by a new environment! I intend soon to devote myself to the affairs of next summer; at any moment I am ready to attend to any necessary matters, in order to participate to the best of my strength and ability in the worries left to you.

Greet your dear wife cordially from us both; our departure was beautiful and quite in keeping with our first meeting.

In sincere friendship,

RICHARD WAGNER.

Fidi [1] took the whip away from the coachman to-day because he always beat his horses.

## To FRIEDRICH FEUSTEL

(SORRENTO, October 7, 1876.)

*Dearest Friend!*

Best greetings first of all to my good friends of the Executive Council! Next, sincere thanks,

---

[1] Fidi was the pet name of Siegfried Wagner.

and a humble plea for pardon, for my previous silence.

Until to-day I have had no leisure, but now I shall set about fulfilling my obligations one by one. For to-day only information as to plans. First of all, I consider an appeal to the patrons as indispensable.

To procure a loan for an undertaking which was regarded with universal suspicion was quite a different thing from securing energetic co-operation and support for one which, to the astonishment of the whole world, has been carried into effect.

Very naturally, however, this co-operation is to be effected only from a small number of genuine enthusiasts, who are at the same time men of means.

The appeal which I have drawn up for this purpose I am sending first of all to you, in order that the report of the Executive Council may be added.

In addition to this appeal I intend to make

application to some of the most distinguished patrons with the request that they head a subscription list, to be sent out by them personally. For this I have Count Magnis particularly in view, as he has already declared himself willing; however, I shall put myself in touch with Herr v. Radowitz in order, if possible, to form a committee at once.

I further intend to ask the advice of my friends as to whether or not I shall apply to the Emperor for reimbursement.

Perhaps only a suggestion would be necessary to explain to him that, in addition to distributing orders to the assisting musicians, my efforts should meet with direct personal recognition.

By this I naturally mean nothing less than aid in meeting the expenses, the burden of which should not be allowed to fall upon me. This done, the way would possibly be opened for me to lay a petition before Parliament asking for the further support of the Bayreuth Festival Play as a national project. Some time will be necessary

to work this out, but fortunately we still have
plenty of time at our disposal, as we shall not
be together and ready for business before
November.

The King wrote me quite splendidly while I
was in Venice, exhorting me to endurance and
perseverance, which he places above everything
else. I hope accordingly to see everything settled before the close of the year, and hope to
begin the preparation for the repetition of the
Festival by the beginning of the new year. This
latter requires much self-control on my part, as
I shall feel myself compelled to proceed very
seriously and strictly in improving both the *personnel* and the performance, especially if I find
the proper sympathy and support. At present
all courage and desire to make such an effort
are totally lacking.

For two days I have been in Sorrento, our
temporary goal; we are quite delighted with the
place, only we shall be obliged to enter upon some
agreement with the hotel, as otherwise our stay

here will be so tremendously expensive. Unfortunately there was no one to help us in finding good accommodations, and we were obliged to secure everything with the greatest difficulty.

So think of us then ever kindly, dearest friend! Remember us cordially to your dear family; assure our friends of our faithful devotion, and believe always in the sincere gratitude of

Your deeply devoted

RICHARD WAGNER.

The first Festival closed with a deficit of $37,500, and Wagner was forced to admit that persistence in the plan was nothing short of reckless, as not more than half the number of Patrons' Certificates necessary to cover the actual expenses had been subscribed. A few weeks after the Festival he went with his family to Italy, thus carrying out the intention to which he gave expression on the occasion of the *fête* arranged in honour of his sixty-third birthday:

"When this nonsense is all over, I intend to

stretch myself out at full length, presumably in Italy, and there, with wife and child, to thrive upon the money received from my American march."

But he was not able to escape the haunting thought of the burden created by the deficit.

In November he sent out a circular letter to the patrons of the Festival asking for renewed assistance under the supposition that they had made his cause their own and would now stand by him in his hour of direct need. But his confidence was rudely shaken by the meagreness of the response, and he could only come to the conclusion that there had been " in reality no patrons at all, but only spectators occupying expensive seats." Thus the burden of the deficit rested practically upon him, and Finck says with fine irony:

" He had composed and presented to his contemporaries an immortal work of art; now he was called upon to pay for it, and was, moreover, soundly taken to task by the press for not having thanked these contemporaries for going to hear it."

## To Emil Heckel

(Sorrento, November 3, 1876.)

*My dearest Friend Heckel!*

You are really the first person in Germany from whom a sign of life has come. Accept my thanks for this.

As yet Herr Feustel has let nothing be heard from himself but the most terrifying reports about the increasing deficit, in covering which it is claimed that I am the only one who can save the situation. Good! I have framed my appeal and sent it out; I have made inquiries in Berlin and also of the King of Bavaria without having received an answer.

Your idea of having a fourth performance to cover the deficit is, under the wretched conditions, certainly the most feasible; however, the payment of certain debts cannot be postponed so long.

As I hear nothing at present but distressing news in connection with the closing of the Festival, and as I feel just now that very great encouragement for the repetition and continuation of the Festival must be given me, if I am to overcome my unbounded repugnance for the entire matter, I am only waiting for some particularly painful experience to occur which would decide me to retreat entirely, and I wish this to be interpreted in the most literal sense. I shall then remain silent, and without a murmur give whatever there is to the creditors of the undertaking, just as would be the case with a legal bankrupt.

Really, you are the only one — yes, the sole one — who shows serious solicitude about me in the matter!

Under such circumstances my health cannot be of the best, my mental suffering and this agony of uncertainty are too great. On the other hand, I am able to rejoice over the good health of my wife and children in these beautiful surroundings. . . . However, we shall soon be obliged to turn our faces homeward, as my private treasury was so exhausted last summer (in spite of the American March) that it will not suffice to keep us here much longer.

Therefore! Most cordial greetings from Wagner's to Heckel's.

Yours faithfully,

RICHARD WAGNER.

This letter is in answer to one in which Heckel informs Wagner that the Executive Council had decided against the publication of a circular appealing for assistance in covering the deficit. "It is *our* affair to decide upon ways and means, and I am of the opinion that this should be done by personal letters and visits to the real friends of the undertaking." Heckel had also conceived the idea of giving four instead of three performances of the " Ring " in 1877, the receipts of the extra cycle to be applied to covering the deficit.

For three years, instead of applying the receipts of his concerts to his private exchequer,

Wagner had borne all the expense of the costly trips and hotel bills. It was undoubtedly this pressure on his private purse which led him to accept a curious offer which came to him from America.

This was an invitation to write a festival composition, in the form of a march, for the formal opening of the Centennial in Philadelphia. The idea of intrusting this music to the greatest living composer originated with Theodore Thomas, who was at that time the conductor of the New York Philharmonic Society.

The suggestion met with ready response, and the Woman's Society of the Centennial Committee pledged themselves to raise the necessary funds. Wagner had resolutely rejected previous overtures of this sort, and in acceding to this one he was undoubtedly influenced by two reasons — the more immediate one that of retrieving his financial embarrassment, and, as a more remote one, the hope of interesting Americans in his great Bayreuth enterprise.

Of this he leaves no doubt, as he distinctly writes: " If I send it to you, I shall then expect the Americans to treat me well, particularly in regard to advancing the interests of my Festival."

Upon receiving a second invitation through Theodore Thomas, Wagner declared himself willing to write a composition for large orchestras of the character of the Kaiser March, and to send it to any German banking-house which might be chosen, in return for which he was to receive the sum of five thousand dollars.

The result was the splendid Centennial March, which Americans of the older generation heard and wondered at without realising the true greatness of the genius who had written it, and what his reformatory ideas were to signify to the art world.

The motto he chose was the Goethe line: " Nur der verdient sich Freiheit wie das Leben, der täglich sie erobern muss." ("He only merits freedom as well as life who must daily conquer them.")

This word "erobern" (to conquer) led to a comical misunderstanding; the delegates sent to receive the composition could speak but little German, and Wagner less English. One of them translated the word to mean " to rob," and Wagner often laughed heartily at this unexpected version of the Goethe lines.

A curious point in connection with this composition was that, for the first time in his life, the imperative need of executing a work was there before the poetic idea had taken form. This lack of inspiration was due to the fact that his musical spirit was soaring in the more rarefied region of the " Parsifal " music instead of being devoted to his American patrons. Anton Seidl relates that Wagner was genuinely depressed for a time by his vain search for a theme on which to build his march, until one day, as he stepped out of a dark passage into the bright sunlight, the Goethe motto, as well as the opening theme in triplets, suddenly came to him.

The soft lyric passages of the work, by his

own confession, were written with the "beautiful and clever women of North America in mind."

When a telegram came from America reporting the success of the work, he said whimsically:

"Do you know what the best thing about that march is?  The money that I got for it!"


## To Friedrich Feustel

*Esteemed Friend!*                (Rome, November 23, 1876.)

Since my departure from Bayreuth, no further information has reached me than your announcement that the deficit proves to be more and more significant, and that I am expected to suggest ways and means of meeting it.  To me the most imperative thing seemed to be an appeal to the previous supporters of my undertaking.  I drew up such an appeal and sent it to you (about the 8th or 10th of October) with the request that your report to the patrons be added to it.  At the same time I wrote at length to the King of Bavaria and enclosed the chief features of a plan for a constitution, by the terms of which the theatre with all     accessories should accrue to the state in exchange of the assumption of all the debts resting upon it, and the further administration of which should be transferred to the city magistrate of Bayreuth. Up to the present time no answer has reached me, and I can only assume that the King is not lacking in cordial good-will, but that he is embarrassed in finding just the right way of meeting my wishes.

While I was waiting for an answer from that side, my friend Heckel announced to me his great regret that I myself should be called upon to make the appeal for a contribution to cover the deficit, whereas, to his mind, this should be the affair of my friends; this opinion he had already expressed to our friends of the Executive Council. I answered that he seemed to be moved by a very proper feeling, and that it would indeed be gratifying to me if the matter could be taken in hand by friends of my cause. In regard to his suggestion that four (extra) performances at increased prices should be given to cover the deficit, I expressed the fear that the imperative payment of our debts could not be postponed for so long a period.

I am convinced that there are people who can and will gladly get together the necessary funds for us; however, I do not know anyone of the proper ability who could be asked to place himself at the head and front of such a movement.

Perhaps this could be accomplished by the committees of the older Wagner Societies, for whom it would surely be easier to raise their voices now than at a time when the undertaking was received with suspicion on all sides.

In any case, I regret that no use was made of the appeal I sent to you; at least one good result would have come from its distribution in letting us know where we stood in the matter.

It seems to me that through no fault of mine there has been much unnecessary delay; on the other hand, I declare myself still ready to support any measure which is suggested to me.

Under all these circumstances it seems now to have grown too late to prepare for a repetition of the Festival next summer with any degree of assurance — in fact, even to entertain such an idea. In order to reach the goal *once*, and to show the world what it was all about, I could enter into these financial embarrassments and deceptions; but to remain continually in such a condition by exposing myself repeatedly to the chance of being abandoned to fresh anxieties (for example, through the calumny of the newspapers), of which I should never have even learned, as no financial profit was ever connected with my undertaking — all this I must absolutely refuse to do in the future.

The great defects in the performance of my work can only be explained by the financial uncertainty and the consequent doubts which arose as to the timely accomplishment of the undertaking on the part of those commissioned with its execution. We shall be obliged to have at our immediate disposal the means for remedying these defects.  Moreover, I should not have the courage to approach certain artists of my *personnel*, whom I secured only with the greatest difficulty, and invite them to renewed co-operation without being able to assure them of an adequate honorarium; this, however, could not be done unless the deficit of this year's performances had been previously completely covered. And to give a fourth (extra performance) for this purpose would naturally fill the minds of any singers and musicians with consternation as soon as they heard of it, for it would be tempting Providence to rely solely upon a repetition of the auspicious circumstances which made it possible for us to give the three performances successively within so short a time.

I am therefore obliged to wait and see if by any impulse whatever the money for covering the deficit can be collected in time.  Has this not been done by January 1st, then a repetition of the Festival next year must be abandoned, and then we can only wait and see if any interest is taken in the matter in certain quarters and help is extended to us. I refrain from any reference to my own person on this occasion, nor shall I call your attention in detail to the state of my health. I only assure you that even here in Italy, under the influence of totally new impressions, I drag along with my entire nervous system apparently shattered; nor is this to be wondered at when one considers that I have been prevented from taking my customary water-cure, in spite of all things that have happened and continue to happen. Moreover, I cannot regard the absolute necessity of the repetition of the Festival next year as obligatory for me, unless this can take place under such circumstances as to make a pleasant duty of the self-sacrifices it would incur — that is, if the friends of my art do not convince me that they care something about me and my undertaking. I can and will not sacrifice my strength any more to a mere enterprise, for better for worse.

As not the slightest blame in this deplorable

situation is to be laid at the door ot my esteemed friends in Bayreuth — we having mutually accomplished something that was able to arouse astonishment and enthusiasm — it is all the more painful to be obliged to prepare you, in an extreme case, for the most depressing news.

I must look squarely in the face the possibility that we shall never be able to have another Festival performance, and this state of things would occur if the deficit could not be covered at the given time, and at the same time the payments could no longer be postponed. In this case nothing would remain but to declare the undertaking in a state of bankruptcy, and all existing property, after a report to this effect to the patrons, would be turned over to our creditors.

Whatever belongs to the King of Bavaria would be made over to him, and whatever else of value remained be sold to the highest bidder, and the money applied to discharging the remaining debts. For my part, I see no other course to take, as I am forced to doubt exceedingly any further success as the result of my personal efforts, and no one who is acquainted with the strain I have been under would expect me to give concerts and the like at present.

Above all, most esteemed friend, do not interpret this communication as the outburst of a despondent man who is trying to disquiet you in a most terrible manner; on the contrary, I have had ample opportunity of considering my real attitude toward my contemporaries during the past ten months and have accordingly reached this conclusion. I have shown what I can do, and feel myself justified, as well as impelled, to close my artistic career, and regard as my sole duty henceforth the welfare of my friends and my family, which has hitherto been sacrificed (to the success of the undertaking).

With the most cordial greetings to the friends and family, I remain

Your always grateful and devoted

RICHARD WAGNER.

## To Friedrich Feustel

(Rome, November 29, 1876.)

*Much esteemed Friend!*

I regret that you did not acquaint me with the delay in the distribution of my circular to the patrons, in which case I could then have informed you how the appeal it contained could have even most effectively disseminated, without being accompanied by the report of the Executive Committee.

I beg of you to retrieve this delay as quickly as possible by sending out the appeal in the form of a letter to my patrons.

As I look at the matter, this step is the only one which it remains for me to take in order to proclaim the true state of affairs; in my earlier letter, of which only the last clause seems to have made any impression upon you, I informed you that all my previous efforts had remained without any results.

In this letter I also assured you of my willingness to take any step suggested by you or other friends in securing the necessary assistance; to proceed, however, to announce a repetition of the Festival after such serious delay was a step which I did not feel myself justified in taking.

In considering the latter hypothesis I did not overlook the fact that, if no help came from the outside towards covering the deficit, the remaining debts would become so urgent that the settlement of them would have to be considered from the ordinary standpoint of civic law.

I had nothing more or less in mind concerning the prospective bankruptcy process than the payment of these debts by the sale of the property.

In doing this, it did not occur to me to keep the carpenters and paperers of Bayreuth out of their money, and if I used the word "bankrupt" in this connection, it was only to characterise unreservedly my position, as I do not hesitate to declare myself and my artistic undertaking as completely bankrupt.

On the contrary, I should like to see my residence in Bayreuth, as well as my private income, — in regard to which you are able to give the most accurate information, — appropriated to the liquidation of the debts, and I beg of you not to entertain the slightest doubt on this point.

I thought I had intimated this to you when I announced my intention, under extreme circumstances, of relinquishing my artistic career and devoting myself only to the interests of my family, who must be regarded as heavy sufferers.

With the most respectful greetings,

Your ever grateful

RICHARD WAGNER.

## To FRIEDRICH FEUSTEL

(FLORENCE, December 4, 1876.)

*Dear Friend!*

I thank you very much for the recent favourable news.  The circular, of which (also with thanks) I am sending you at once a revised copy, I beg of you in any case to have sent out as quickly as possible to my patrons. I must have this as a basis for further proceedings. I intend to stop in Munich for further conference, and declare to you further that I have left nothing undone to make possible the *barely imaginable* case of a repetition of the performances next summer.

Only here in Florence have I been able to arrange for the end of my visit in Italy, as I could not refuse the worthy Bolognese to be present at the last performance of " Rienzi." *Everything* pleased me very much, even though it was a very great strain. . . .

In any case we expect to celebrate the Christmas Festival at home.

I beg of you to convey my most cordial greetings to your valued family and our friends.

Ever gratefully mindful of your friendship,

Yours faithfully,

RICHARD WAGNER.

Heckel was obliged to agree with Feustel that it was an unfavourable moment to launch a fresh appeal to the patrons, and felt it to be his duty to inform Wagner of this. The latter was very much agitated and wrote the following letter to Heckel:

(FLORENCE, December 9, 1876).

*Dear Friend!*

I am very sorry that you also have the heart to give me and my concerns no furthe consideration, and only speak to me of the matter in the same strain as do my other friends. No person is able to devise ways and means; even my appeal to the patrons should be sent only " with caution," because the times are so bad, and yet, notwithstanding this, the performances should be announced as quickly as possible! It is incredible! You inquire, in fact, about the Festival medallion, which I naturally countermanded at once, when the ever-increasing deficit was announced. What does one *not* expect of me!

For my part, I announce to you quite positively

that I shall devote the coming summer entirely to regaining my health — for which, on account of my increasing abdominal trouble, I expect to take a protracted water-cure in November.

If I find myself restored to health, we shall then see what can be arranged for the year after next. If in the meantime the deficit is not covered, and this without further effort on my part, I intend to hand the theatre over to some enterprising person, possibly even to the Munich Royal Theatre, but not to give myself any further concern about it. Here, dear friend, my strength is exhausted. My undertaking up to this point has been a question to the German public — " Will you? " I now assume that they will not, and accordingly am at the end of my resources. I beg you to consider the matter from now on solely in this light, and, if you think it wise, also to explain summarily to my other friends about me, as they seem unable to understand.

In one of my constant‧ sleepless nights I am

seeking to create for myself some degree of comfort by unburdening my heart frankly and freely to the true and sympathetic friend, as which I have ever recognised you.

Remain kindly disposed to me!

Yours ever faithfully,

RICHARD WAGNER.

# WAYS AND MEANS

## 1877–1879

### To Emil Heckel

(Bayreuth, February 11, 1877.)

*Oh! dearest, dearest Friend!*

Yes, yes! The King of Bavaria! As if that could make up to me for the time that has been lost!

Do you not believe that if anyone could do it, I am that one, and do you think that I have not done my utmost?

Please let us be silent on this point!

You must have realised, dear friend, that what I have now set in motion has only been done in order to preserve the honour of my undertaking and my attitude toward the same.

On the other hand, do you really believe that I ever had any hope that anything would be accomplished?

Learn to know Germany and the German public! That is all — all lost! Believe me!

What we accomplished last year was a miracle, and will remain so, as long as anyone knows about it. But beyond that it will never, never go: this we must realise once for all.

The performances for this year are already impossible, both from material and artistic reasons; even if the money could be obtained, it would not suffice; the artistic dangers are great. A resumption could only be thought of if my programme in regard to a Patrons' Society (but not alone on the basis of the former allotment plan) could be strictly carried out. The new one must have quite a different aspect from the old; there must be power and knowledge behind it.

In the meantime I have to look after the deficit, and intend therefore to give concerts in England several months, solely for this purpose. If I return alive, I hope nothing further will be required of me than to think of myself — to recover and — forget!

Well, we are so far!

Now, dear friend, get His Majesty the King of Bavaria out of your head, and continue to be kindly disposed to your

Ever faithful

RICHARD WAGNER.

TO EMIL HECKEL

(BAYREUTH, April 11, 1877.)

*My dear Heckel!*

God grant you long life, at least decidedly longer than mine, in order that someone will be there after my death who in himself shall furnish a root for further cultivation.

I understand everything, but say little — if possible, no more — about it. I can do nothing but wait until someone from the outside follows after, as I seem to be considerably in advance!

Cordial greetings!

Yours,

RICHARD WAGNER.

In January the King's Councillor arrived in Bayreuth to discuss the matter of the deficit with Wagner and the gentlemen of the Executive Council.

Should the King or the German Parliament decide to assume the debt, then Wagner declared his readiness to resume the Festival performances in 1878.  His second suggestion was that the King should take over the Bayreuth Theatre as a sort of adjunct to the Munich opera until the loan was discharged.

The King's messenger seemed, however, not authorised to accept either of these suggestions, and the conference, from which so much was hoped, left the situation unchanged.

It was while under the shadow of this disappointment that Wagner surprised his wife one day with the announcement: " I shall begin my ' Parsifal ' and not stop until it is finished!"

Everything that had been left sealed up in his innermost soul now began to germinate and reveal itself.  From day to day the earlier sketch of 1865 assumed a firmer and more tangible shape.

Since finishing the " Meistersinger " text, fifteen years before, Wagner the poet had been obliged to recede before Wagner the man of affairs, but that mathematical worries had not destroyed his metrical facility was proven by the rapidity with which the " Parsifal " legend assumed the proportions of a music drama.

During his visit to London in the spring of the same year he was able to read the complete versified text to a select company, including, among other distinguished personalities from the English world of art and letters, George Eliot and her husband, George Henry Lewes.

From London the text went back to his royal benefactor in Munich, whose name had already been mentioned in connection with the " Parsifal " drama in a letter written almost two decades earlier. " He is so strikingly handsome that he might pose as the King of the Jews; and in strict confidence — I am thinking a great deal about the Christian tragedy; possibly something may come of it."

In the meantime, however, the creator of "Parsifal" was being confronted by the stubborn statistics of the Festival deficit, and in order to meet the most urgent part of the indebtedness he had been obliged to borrow the sum of eight thousand dollars at five per cent interest.

Not without extreme reluctance did he yield to the suggestion of August Wilhelmj that he should come to London for a series of Wagnerian concerts, but necessity and a desire to prove to his friends that he had no wish to shirk any responsibility which might give an impetus to the situation finally prevailed over his personal feeling in the matter.

Six concerts were arranged to take place at the Albert Hall, Wagner conducting the first half of each programme, and Hans Richter the second, with the co-operation of a number of the Bayreuth singers. It soon became clear that these concerts would not, as had been expected, wipe out the Bayreuth deficit; for while the audiences were eager, the expenses were so enormous as to cause disaster to the box-office receipts.

At first the actual financial condition was kept from Wagner, but as soon as he learned how matters were going he voluntarily offered to renounce the large sum promised him for his personal services, and moreover paid the singers, whom he had brought with him from Germany, out of his own pocket.

This sacrifice his business agents, Messrs. Hodge and Essex, refused to accept, although they were themselves on the brink of bankruptcy, and the sum of seven hundred pounds was eventually remitted to Bayreuth.

When the disastrous results of the Albert Hall Festival became known, a number of wealthy and public-spirited men determined to wipe off the stain on the English artistic character by opening a subscription list which resulted in the sum of five hundred and sixty pounds.

But Wagner's pride prevented him from accepting from the hands of strangers that which would have been a largesse from his own countrymen, and he accordingly returned the sum to the subscribers.

Apart from George Eliot and her husband, Wagner also made the acquaintance of Robert Browning and Burne-Jones and saw Joseph Jefferson in his famous characterisation of Rip Van Winkle.

Henry T. Finck includes in his Wagner biography Mr. Hubert Herkomer's amusing account of how he painted his famous portrait for the German Athenæum Club:

" The whole business of the portrait was disagreeable to him, but I was at least allowed free admission to his abode (12 Orme Street), so this ' seeing ' instead of ' sitting ' went on for nearly a month; my patience was sorely tried, and my independence got chafed.

" But I was wrought up to a curious pitch of excitement during this training, for I was affected by the personal power of the man over those around him, by the magic of his music, and by the face of this poet-musician, which, when stirred by emotion, was a grand reflection of his work.

" Now I doubt whether any man since Napoleon has ever been known to exercise such powers of fascination over his admirers as Richard Wagner does daily, and will do to the termination of his life. You lose your identity when in his presence, and are inclined to forget that there is something else in the world besides Wagner and his music. You are under the influence that sets every nerve at its highest key. He has been able to make people frantic with enthusiasm. . . .

" Wagner was in my mind day and night — a constant vision which barred out every other thought, willing or unwilling — and it was in a moment of anger arising from this constant putting off of the sittings that I determined to try what my memory could furnish, and with his face only inwardly visible to me, I set to work. I worked all day, and it grew I knew not how. The next day I worked still harder and more excitedly and finished the portrait. On the third day I took it to Wagner.

" Up to that time he had but suffered me to be near him, paying little more attention to me than to an animal, but from the moment that he saw his portrait his demeanour changed, and never did a man show admiration more truly and heartily than did Richard Wagner on this occasion, and ever since to me.

" How I had done it puzzled him. You use ' witchcraft,' he said to me.

" So then he was ready to sit for me, and I was intensely eager, not to say nervous, to compare my impressional portrait with the original subject."

To FRIEDRICH FEUSTEL

(LONDON, May 13, 1877.
12 Orme Square,
Bayswater,
W. London.)

*Dearest Friend!*

In addition to the communication made to friend Adolph, I have nothing further to say in regard to the conditions here. If, in spite of my accurate knowledge of these conditions which has always kept me from visiting London, I could have entertained the thought that perhaps, this once, such an effort might be successful (unheard of!), it was, on the whole, not so much this idea and the hope based upon it which induced me to come to London, as the resolve to prove to you and the friends in favour of this plan, that it was neither laziness nor love of ease on my part which led me to hope that the deficit might be met in some other way.

It is now time to take another course, and therefore I beg of you in the most friendly spirit to send out at once an appeal from the Executive Council of the Stage Festival Play enterprise for a subscription to cover the deficit; in this you will kindly recapitulate the state of affairs, and also mention my zeal in endeavouring to spare the patrons this burden by the most importunate efforts. At the same time I shall ask you to open the list with a subscription of three thousand marks *from me*, to which you may also feel inclined to add a subscription as a generous private citizen.

I should not care to have the circulars put into the hands of the Wagner Societies as such, on account of their great impotence, but recommended to a few private persons. . . . As soon as the lists are full, and strong enough to meet our needs, the complete list had better be sent at once to each subscriber with a request for payment. Should this course also fail, then I have resolved to close with Ullmann for America, to offer my Bayreuth property for sale, and go across the ocean with my entire family, never to return to Germany.

As far as the local business here is concerned, we fear that we shall not even make our expenses. I should be glad if the money I advanced to the singers through you could be returned to me. In any case you would greatly oblige me by placing a sum to my credit here in order that I might be able to move comfortably to Ems the beginning of June.

As to whether or not my health is restored will depend largely upon the character of the news I receive as to the start and progress of the subscription list.

It is to be hoped that something comforting will happen from this side!

Bear with me and forgive the many anxieties I have caused you. Remember us cordially to our friends, your dear family, and especially my good Adolph.

Your ever grateful

RICHARD WAGNER.

TO FRIEDRICH FEUSTEL

(LONDON, May 27, 1877.<br/>Sunday, early.)

*Dearest Friend!*

It seems now as if I am destined to hear of calamity on top of calamity. I read in your — otherwise so highly welcome — communication to Dannreuther that the amount of the deficit is estimated at one hundred and sixty thousand marks; in our conversation concerning the possible London receipts, you specified the sum necessary for covering the deficit at five thousand pounds; I have never known of anything more than "something" over one hundred thousand marks.

If the deficit in the meantime is really swollen by fifty or sixty thousand marks, then I must confess that with this continued obscurity as to my obligations my last particle of courage forsakes me, and I prefer to give myself up to desperation.

I deduce some little hope for the success of the last projected subscription from the fact that I see more and more clearly that my deep discouragement as to the complete failure of my appeal to the patrons of last year was without cause.

I showed Dannreuther a copy of that appeal which you sent me lately as an intimation of the failure of the more recent effort, and learned to my astonishment that he knew nothing whatever of that appeal; as we have heard the same from various sources, we can only attribute this enigmatic circumstance to some singular mishap in sending it out.

If a similar ill fate does not control this renewed effort, may it bring us better and more encouraging information as to the true attitude of our friends!

Forgive the cursoriness of these lines! Heartily thanking you for all the care and solicitude which your active friendship impels you to assume for me, I greet you most cordially as

Your ever devoted

RICHARD WAGNER.

To-morrow and the day following, concerts!

To FRIEDRICH FEUSTEL

(LONDON, May 30, 1877.
12 Orme Square,
Bayswater,
W. London.)

*Most valued Friend!*

I suffer greatly by your conduct. The caution you employ leads me to infer that you consider our representation of my position in London as exaggerated, and that you imagine we should be able to help ourselves, while the chief thing for you is to make payments in Bayreuth.

If no further help comes, then I am resolved to surrender everything to which I have the least shadow of a title. I desire that no attempt shall be made to dissuade me from doing this. I need the London money *for London*, in order that I may not appear as a bankrupt. Everything I have experienced here is confirmed with my former knowledge of London; and yet, in spite of this, I sacrificed my better views to you in order not to appear indolent and unwilling.

I leave quite out of the question how much older I have grown under these renewed experiences, and how much vitality I have squandered in vain. This and that will still be tried here, and a local subscription will probably bring in something; but for the present I beg you to take my explanations and wishes quite seriously and not bring me to a point of desperation by opposing them.

Forgive these lines! But I cannot do otherwise!

With the most respectful greetings,

Your ever grateful

RICHARD WAGNER.

This letter was followed by a telegram the next day saying:

Erroneous report regarding size of deficit led me into violence in letter, which regret and beg you to forgive.

WAGNER.

To FRIEDRICH FEUSTEL

(LONDON, June 3, 1877.)

*Dearest Friend!*

At last the confusion of the past few days begins to unravel itself! I am astonished how difficult it is to obtain accuracy even from clear-headed business men.

I shall report to you in time verbally into what

a state of perplexity I have been thrown by incredible thoughtlessness and ignorance, as well as fantastic presumption not based on reality. Enough! No one has lost a penny by me or through me.

I send you herewith a cheque for seven hundred pounds, and beg you to place me on the subscription list with ten thousand marks, and to pay this sum at once to the most pressing creditor — the remainder of the London receipts to be placed at my disposal.

The result of the London subscription will be made known to us in a short time.

Now, don't be angry with me for my recent violence. It was really high time the singers should be paid; and the twelve hundred pounds was to be employed first of all for this purpose.

It was announced to me that only twelve thousand marks had been returned by you, and that the bank would not pay this to me without your *special* instruction.

The first report (incorrect) caused the letter;

the second, the telegram. I soon perceived the error in regard to the size of your remittance.

Therefore I beg for written absolution! I have reached the extreme point and could literally jump out of my skin at any moment. . . .

I thank you warmly for the good birthday wish; it delighted me greatly (on this gloomy day).

To-morrow evening we start for Ems, where we expect to arrive on the evening of the 5th. Only Adolph knows the address; I do not.

Kindest and best greetings from us to you and yours.

Your ever grateful

RICHARD WAGNER.

## To FRIEDRICH FEUSTEL

(EMS, June 14, 1877.)

*Dearest Friend!*

Here are the two signatures! May this encroachment upon the real existence of my family at least serve to gain time enough in which to

learn in peace and quiet how matters stand, and
with what kind of people I shall have to deal
throughout my life.   In order to see clearly for
the future, I feel myself obliged to recognise that
it is not my work which has been censured but
— Bayreuth.

My works will be performed everywhere and
attract numerous spectators, but no one will come
to Bayreuth.

This is the real state of the case, and the cause
of the intervening coolness for my enterprise.
I can blame the place only in so far that I chose
it.   And yet I had a great idea in so doing; I
hoped, with the support of the nation, to create
a thoroughly new and independent work in a
place which should first rise to importance
through this work — a sort of Art-Washington.

I had too high an opinion of our best society.
In order to please me, and at the same time to
satisfy their curiosity, they sacrificed themselves
once to the terrible inconvenience of Bayreuth,
but became frightened when a repetition was

suggested.    Therefore the coolness toward my enterprise.   A very important London firm communicated to me an offer to remove the Bayreuth stage machinery to a big London theatre, with a repetition of the Festival during the whole of next season.   If I *really* wished it, a theatre like mine will be built for me in Leipzig, and Würzburg or Nuremberg, to judge by the great success of the preceding year, would be able to compensate me and continue the work. Bayreuth can only be a success if my idea of a musical and dramatic high school, which I recently pointed out, could be carried into effect, as this would lead to distinguished people settling there.   The city itself, which would reap great profit, could present a petition to the King, etc.

As far as I am concerned, I shall probably do nothing more than worry myself to death to cover the deficit and get rid of the theatre!

I am frightened anew at hearing of the manner in which the twenty thousand marks recently received in Vienna has melted away to seven thousand nine hundred.

*Dolce far niente* — yes, yes! Do *nothing!* — No: *accomplish* nothing! that is my vocation.

Now, as God wills! I remain under everlasting obligations to you!

Cordial greetings from

Your devoted

RICHARD WAGNER.

"The two signatures" mentioned in the opening of this letter were those placed by Wagner and his wife to a legal document empowering Feustel to draw a certain sum from their private treasury and expend it in satisfying the demands of the most urgent creditors. This, together with the sum which he had renounced in London in order to pay the singers he had taken with him from Germany, amounted to about fifty thousand marks.

To Friedrich Feustel

(Ems, July 2, 1877.)

*Dear Friend!*

If you are still alive, I will not delay in acquainting you with my immediate travelling plans. . . .

I have announced myself for the third week of the month in Munich (His Majesty has already written me very graciously). Will you accordingly be kind enough to arrange for our meeting there!

Should any change of plans occur, you will be informed in good time. I hope that all is well with you and your family. Every move or retreat on the chessboard of life brings anger with it, which undoubtedly arises from the fact that most persons are very sordid.

Under the circumstances of the " present," it must be regarded as a " matter of course " that we were obliged to spend our last spare penny to pay the claims of the Bayreuth hotel-keepers last year.

Heckel was here; he will get as far as theatre-director in Mannheim — so now at least he has something from it! I now hope — and really hope — to be able to shift my heavy burden upon the Munich Royal Theatre.

This is the last hope of my strange life!

Therefore we shall see each other soon. Think kindly of me in the meantime.

I am going to learn to play Taroc[1] soon! Cordial greetings to the entire *Feustelei!*

Ever your grateful<br>RICHARD WAGNER.


To EMIL HECKEL

(Telegram)

(HEIDELBERG, July 7, 1877.)

Please take dinner with us to-morrow at one o'clock with Zeroni. In the evening reading of " Parsifal," to which Pastor also invited.

WAGNER.

---

[1] A well-known Bavarian game of cards.

Of this meeting Heckel writes:

" In addition to Zeroni, myself, and the Catholic priest, Richard Pohl came from Baden-Baden. We were the first who were made acquainted with the drama of ' Parsifal.' It is indescribable with what feeling and deep emotion the Master read us his own poem. He was so moved that he withdrew after the reading and left us alone.

" We also remained silent, and it was a long time before we felt ourselves again on this crooked earth ! "

In Heidelberg Richard Wagner and General Grant met, but the meeting was not very satisfactory, as the distinguished warrior had never conquered either German or French.

## To Friedrich Feustel

(Bayreuth, October 9, 1877.)

*Dearest Friend!*

In order to prove the vitality of our entire project it seems to me to be high time to begin with the advertisements for applications.

In regard to Hey we shall be obliged to come to some conclusion, and this can only appear justifiable when we shall have been given our cue to a certain extent by the success of the announcement in regard to the school.

Therefore — in haste — advertise! or: have you any doubts then: hold back entirely! What do you think?

I was on my way to you, but my bad toe forced me to turn back.

Cordial greetings from

Your ever devoted

RICHARD WAGNER.

Defeated in his plan of repeating the " Ring," Wagner's active brain at once evolved a bigger general scheme, which was to make the Bayreuth Theatre a Dramatic High School, where singers, players, and conductors could learn to interpret not only the Wagnerian works but all of the classics in a correct manner.

He counted upon the co-operation of Liszt,

Wilhelmj, and Professor Julius Hey, the distinguished Munich singing-master. He hoped that under his personal guidance and inspiration this idea would ripen into a stable foundation for future Bayreuth deeds, and he rejoiced in the added significance that would be given to his beloved Bayreuth by such a concentration of the various artistic elements. He wrote to Wilhelmj:

" I have in my mind to teach the young people something before I die; namely, *tempo* — that is to say, interpretation. Could you assure me of your assistance here in Bayreuth from January 1 to April 20 for quartette playing and general higher analytical interpretation. What would you demand for this?

" Under no circumstances should I presume or wish to teach *how* it should be done (composing), but only to give instructions as to how that which has already been created should be properly understood and interpreted."

Wagner's idea was to arrange a six-year cycle, which was to include the most significant works

in German musical literature as well as the
Wagner dramas, from the " Flying Dutchman "
to the " Ring," with " Parsifal " as a finale in
1883.

The rehearsals were to take place during the
first two quarters of the year, Wagner himself
to be present at least three times a week. During the third quarter the performances were to
take place.

For the purpose of carrying out this broadly
outlined Festival plan, a central Bayreuth Society of Patrons was formed, each member of
which pledged himself to pay fifteen marks a
year to cover the expenses.

He applied once more to Parliament. Inas-
much as the government paid large sums each
year to institutions of various kinds, why should
not a real dramatic school like the one planned in
Bayreuth receive support as well? The sum of
twenty-five thousand dollars would have been
sufficient, but before the close of the year he
realised the hopelessness of his plans and directed

his friends to concentrate all of their energies in the organisation of a Society of Patrons with a view to making possible the " Parsifal " performance.

As an " equivalent," as Wagner expressed it, for the abandonment of the Dramatic High School, he then proposed a journal which was to be called the " Bayreuther Blätter," and become the organ of communication to the Wagner Societies, a publication which has survived its founder.

That which gives historic significance to the " Bayreuther Blätter " is that in its columns appeared nearly all of the essays which Wagner wrote during the last six years of life, on the greatest possible variety of topics.

### To Friedrich Feustel

(BAYREUTH, February 3, 1878.)

*Dearest Friend!*

I return the Vienna letter to you with many thanks.  We must discuss it again sometime.

But for to-day, dear friend, I wish to express my thanks *to you*, for the extraordinary patience, wisdom, and energy which you have employed in dealing with the situation in regard to the Festival deficit, and to express my great joy that, although this has been accomplished through the King's noble friendship for me, it is your efforts which have led up to such satisfactory results.

The turn in our affairs is all the more comforting to me, as it is, in reality, owing to the unexpected success of my own work that we now find ourselves provided with means with which to struggle against the lamentable material results of the year 1876. That is creditable.

But it will depend only upon your confidence in the matter, that, out of the friendly decision of the King, a prompt and genuine solution of the painful situation can be found.

All of this I know, and recognise distinctly, and therefore express to you the most sincere gratitude of a friend.

The chief gain in all this is that I shall now

be able to devote myself with calm imperturba-
bility to new creations, which must be uninterrupted and undisturbed or else the good spirits
take instant flight from us queer " geniuses."

Accept my thanks now and always!

Yours faithfully,

RICHARD WAGNER.


In spite of all the efforts made in various
sources, the covering of the deficit of the first
Stage Festival Play fell upon the creator of this
work.    No effective alliance of patrons and
friends was organised to remove this burden
from him, and nothing remained to be done but
to apply the royalties of the Munich performance
of the " Ring " to the gradual liquidation of the
debt, which meant that not only the funds for
this purpose came from Wagner's private purse,
but that he saw himself coerced into giving up
the pivotal motive of his entire life, namely, the
Bayreuth monopoly of the " Ring."

## To Emil Heckel

(Bayreuth, March 23, 1879.)

*My oldest and most esteemed Friend!*

How could you give me greater pleasure than by the good news that the preparations for the Mannheim performance of the " Ring " are progressing so satisfactorily!

If one takes a closer view of the situation, it seems like a miracle! Fate has taken its *own* course with my works; even though it is not the one which I originally had in view, it behooves me to look on quite soberly and calmly and see what can be accomplished for my cause in this way.

This is my standpoint: I look on from a distance, rejoice over good results, and am not astonished at bad. But — I can never again be present. If you ever learn that I have ever been present at the performance of a part of that work, you will be at liberty to accuse me of treacherous friendship, but such a thing will never happen.

Therefore my most sincere thanks for the kind invitation to Mannheim, which I beg you also to convey to the esteemed gentlemen of Grand Ducal Theatre committee.

Filled with the most agreeable memories of your zeal for my work and its execution, I am and remain

Yours most faithfully,

RICHARD WAGNER.

TO EMIL HECKEL

(BAYREUTH, April 28, 1879.)

*My dear Friend Heckel!*

At last I find time in which to offer my congratulations to you on your splendid success as well as my joy at the success of your performances.

Until now I was not to be diverted from my finishing touches in the composition of " Parsifal "; this is now completed, and you are the first person in the outside world to whom I address myself.

You have furnished a salutary example in Mannheim of what can be accomplished by a powerful will. Since I have been obliged to relinquish all idea of a repetition in Bayreuth, it is only by the most carefully prepared performances in our ordinary theatres that the permanent vitality of my work, if it is not to be altogether lost and forgotten, can be proven.

That you approached your voluntary task with apprehension, by anxiously comparing the scope of your own resources with those of the very largest Royal theatres, decided you to go ahead and follow out my principle of getting at the spirit of the thing. A director who is thoroughly initiated and who is, moreover, intelligent and energetic, and, above all, convinced — such a director, I say, furnishes me with the surest guarantee.

However much as I am pleased at the public praise of Fischer, I am not surprised. I knew what he could do.

It is a great good fortune that I have finally a theatre director who would offer a position to one of the few intelligent and well-trained conductors whom I have succeeded in winning (for my cause).

Until now my recommendations have always proved a detriment to those whom I have recommended; nothing is more odious to the directors of the Royal theatres than the so-called "Wagnerian." For then they say: "Heaven help us! that means a person who will demand a lot of rehearsals, particularly if it is going badly; who, moreover, will not make any cuts, in spite of the fact that it will turn out much better if it is quite incomprehensible. No, indeed! I can get along much better with servile bunglers!" It was better in Mannheim this time, and I hope that the Leipzig performances will also be benefited by the fact that the director there has recently appointed one of my *protégés* — the colleague of Fischer at the Bayreuth performance. And our young Brandt as well!

There is something to be hoped for and expected there — that the entire management, to which I myself am under obligations, will be moved to do the proper thing. Under such circumstances singers and musicians accomplish wonders. I have experienced this. But — the chief wonder of all — Heckel as theatre-director! Good luck! Now I understand fate, and to you, who are in its care, I send cordial greetings.

Yours faithfully,

RICHARD WAGNER.

The *protégé* here mentioned was Anton Seidl, and the director who had the perspicacity sufficient to appoint the young " Wagnerian " was Angelo Neumann, to whom Wagner wrote in this connection:

" You have delighted me by your announcement of Seidl's appointment, because I see from this that there is one theatre at least to which I can be of some service.

" You will never have cause to regret Seidl's

appointment as long as you pursue the course which you have entered.

" Don't concern yourself about anything but giving the *best possible performances*, and if this requires sacrifice, be assured that you will be amply rewarded."

In a previous letter Wagner had recommended his young *protégé* in these words:

" In recommending Seidl to your notice I am consulting his interests less than those of the Leipzig performances of my operas, and — I know what I am doing.

" No one of all the conductors understands so well my *tempi*, and the union of the music with the action. I have trained Seidl. He will conduct the ' Ring ' for you better than anyone else. If my word is not enough to convince you, then I shall never have any further suggestions to make to you."

Neumann, in his recent reminiscences, comments on this letter by saying:

" The Master was quite right in his praise of

Seidl; I was later to find in him the most gifted of all the Wagnerian conductors. . . . I have neither before nor since known a conductor who was able to get such excellent work both from the singers and the musicians. . . .

"Even from soloists of mediocre gifts Seidl succeeded, often in a short time, in securing results which one could expect only from the very first artists. And in addition to this he had a most pronounced instinct and great understanding for scenic arrangements."

In 1885 Seidl was called to New York to succeed Leopold Damrosch as the director of the German opera, and his great services to American art are a matter of too recent history to need any detailed mention here.

He died in New York in 1898.

# PARSIFAL

## ON PREPARATION AND REALISATION

### To Friedrich Feustel

(Naples, March 4, 1880.)

*My dear and faithful Friend!*

You rejoiced me greatly by your very kind letter; accept my best thanks for the same.

The immeasurable sorrow you have had to bear has removed you to a distant and more glorified sphere, and thither I send you my most sympathetic greetings.[1]

My own life has been shrouded in darkness during the past few years; the gray sky which almost incessantly hung heavily above us at home has left its effects not only upon my health but also upon my mental nature.

---

[1] This letter is in response to the news Wagner had received of the death of Feustel's wife.

Frau Cosima Wagner

Had I not had the immeasurable consolation of a family so dear to me, and been surrounded by a few rarely congenial friends, I cannot imagine what could have influenced me to have taken a thought about preserving my own life.

I cherish absolutely no hope for Germany and its conditions, and this is saying a great deal, as, when I entered with full consciousness upon the course I had mapped out for myself, I wrote on my flag, " Stand or fall with Germany! "

For this reason an expensive sojourn in Italy can have absolutely nothing but a climatic significance for me; even this incredible Naples, with all of its life and movement, can serve only as a spectacle for my diversion and to cause me to forget; and even this it cannot really furnish me, as all the misery of our civilisation crowds constantly upon me in a thousand variations of poverty, barbarity, and vice.

In addition to this I have daily increasing cares, that of more and more being unable to meet the growing expenses arising out of my condition, with the means which I have at my command.

In being thus obliged to appeal to you for assistance, I have ever to keep in mind, in view of the rest so imperative for me, how I — to be perfectly frank — shall otherwise be able to manage to exist under the enormous demands made by the state of my health.

I have therefore seriously considered anew a trip to America, and have taken into account the great tax this will make upon my physical strength. To be frank, I have always recoiled from the thought of allowing myself to be dragged about by a speculator only out of avarice, in order that, under the most favourable conditions, I may eventually return with a little fortune and — then begin the misery all over again! — Yes, perhaps, to sacrifice my money again for an idea to which I think I have already sacrificed enough, only to realise in the end how this idea stands in relation to our entire German character.

In spite of this feeling, I must confide to you that the thought of settling permanently in America with my family, my idea, and my work has quite taken possession of me.

I have chiefly to regret that I did not sooner select a fresher and more fertile soil for the future of my works as well as for my family, and therefore my deep conviction of the decadence of European culture only induces me to consider all the more seriously and definitely this means of escape.

I am almost letting my decision depend upon how my offer is regarded by the Americans. At the present I must consider how I may extend my present sojourn, as my excellent local physician strongly recommends the sea baths, which cannot begin before June, as the best remedy for the complete restoration of my health.

This circumstance, which in many ways calls for due consideration, is particularly agreeable to me in one point, and that is the possibility that you and Adolph may visit us here.

*This* would be really something *beautiful* and *worth while*, and believe me, quite apart from the pleasure of our meeting, I long earnestly to show the beauties of this wonder world to those I love; it is indescribable!

My present troubles are nothing but the after effects of the climatic conditions in Bayreuth. Now we are wiser, scarcely leave our terraces and gardens, do not exhaust ourselves with long tours, avoid as far as possible the society and din of the streets, and give up ourselves entirely to the enjoyment of such air and such sunlight as one would rarely find anywhere else on earth — therefore — *Auf Wiedersehen* in Naples!

For to-day I say only a heartfelt fare you well. May you fathom all that I mean thereby.

Always your most grateful friend,

RICHARD WAGNER.

## To Friedrich Schön

(Naples, June 28, 1881.)

*My highly esteemed Friend!*

How deeply I regret to learn from your letter to my dear wife that you are placed in any uncertainty concerning me!

I should like very much to learn, from a plan which you should lay before me, wherein your justification for an agitation in favour of the Bayreuth idea consists, in order that I may do what is expected of me.

I only beg of you, in regard to the execution of your plan, to take into consideration my experience concerning the German world as well as myself.

I should not like you to place my proposed plan of September, 1877, too much in the foreground; as all the experience I have gained serves to show me that at that time — I confess not entirely unconsciously — I reckoned without my host.

If, on the other hand, I take into consideration

the hopes awakened in me and all my friends since you have come to our aid, I can see no other possibility of meeting your wishes than by — as you think — endeavouring to give a fresh impulse to the interest we failed to arouse with the Festival of 1876, by presenting " Parsifal " at the earliest possible moment.

This plan seems feasible for the year 1882, provided I can remain perfectly quiet until that time; but this only, as far as the material possibilities are concerned, in the event that I can lay claim to the assistance of the King of Bavaria.

Under such assured conditions I intend to present, in addition to the " Parsifal," one of my older works each year, in town, making these model performances my artistic testament to my friends.  As I am to-day in my sixty-eighth year, I can count upon a ripe and vigorous old age for the realisation of this plan, and think I shall then have done enough to be released from the performance of " Magic Flute," " Freischütz," " Fidelio," etc.

Anything I can do privately in the way of instruction and information I shall be glad to do — you only need to visit me here in Bayreuth.

If with each performance of my works I do not leave behind my " school," then I have nothing whatever to do with a " school." . . .

## To Carl Brandt

(Bayreuth, January, 1881.)

*Esteemed Friend and Colleague!*

It is going to be serious with " Parsifal." I inquire of you if you are again willing to stand by me. If I have the necessary means, I shall show in yearly performances how I hope to have all of my works performed.

Will you help me in this? We have shown what we can do; *ich muss noch einmal wollen; wollen Sie mit wollen?* [1] If so, then I beg of you as the first thing that you will give me the pleas-

---

[1] It is impossible to find an English equivalent for this reiterative use of the word *wollen*, and in order not to rob it of its intended character, the German phrase is allowed to stand.

ure of a visit as soon as convenient for you; you will be kind enough to stop with me.

With most cordial greetings,

Your faithful old

RICHARD WAGNER.

To EMIL HECKEL

(BAYREUTH, July 2, 1882.)

*Oh! old Friend!*

Must you also make my life a burden by taking offence because I allowed an inquiry from you to be answered by my wife, as it had to be gotten off and I was hard at work on my score?

There seem to be idlers who can always write letters! Possibly I shall come to that also!

Dearest friend, the enclosed I return to you with a thousand thanks (that is understood)! But I cannot possibly bother my patrons with such jests![1]

Many thanks for all your kindness,

Ever your same

RICHARD WAGNER.

[1] Heckel had laboriously arranged an arithmetical table of the number of measures in Wagner's various works which he wished to appear in the "Bayreuther Blätter."

## To Friedrich Feustel

(Venice,
Palazzo Contarini dalle figure,
Gran Canale.)

*My dearest faithful Friend!*

And so a misunderstanding must bring us again into correspondence, after I had refrained for so long a time from approaching you.

The reason for this is to be found in the fact that, after the distressing experience through which you have been called upon to pass, my own situation, at no time free from care and anxiety, did not suggest to me just the way in which this could be done.

Now I know that you yourself have conquered your grief and view life again with firm courage! I was comforted by this!

As for myself, it seems as if nothing could affect me; I see before me possibilities which I have not the least intention of avoiding.

But I am in great perplexity about the offer of this man in Berlin. I believe he is asking for my technical assistance for a Wagner theatre he proposes to erect.

In the meantime I am to build such a theatre upon one of his sites, as a sort of speculation, etc., etc.

For God's sake, let him erect a circus or something of that sort; I have had enough of the Bayreuth theatre.

Will you be kind enough to give this gentleman whatever information you deem necessary?

Something is yet to come of our Bayreuth — at least I think so. My ideas in regard to this you have probably already heard.

1. " Parsifal " I retain solely and exclusively for Bayreuth; even the King renounces it for Munich, but sends me every year his chorus and orchestra.

2. Yearly performances open to everyone for admission (high!).

3. The patrons' fund is to serve as capital for the enterprise; as this fund increases, augmented by the box office receipts, it is in time

to serve for the further performances of my works.

I herewith relinquish all the receipts, as I am not even editing the " Parsifal " score.

I must look elsewhere for personal support; five months in America (September, 1881, April, 1882) shall secure me an independent income.

So the matter stands and — I think all will be well!

Your ever grateful

RICHARD WAGNER.

## To FRIEDRICH FEUSTEL
(BAYREUTH, July 18, 1881.)

*Dearest and most valued Friend!*

After being informed as to the way matters stand in your negotiations as to the publication of a piano arrangement of my Stage-Consecrating Play " Parsifal," I believe it to be necessary to express myself to you in the following manner.

During the writing of the same, the nature of this, my last work, has become more and more clear to me, and I have reached the conclusion that, even under all the circumstances which made possible the performances of single numbers of the " Nibelung's Ring " in our Court and municipal theatres, the Stage-Consecrating Play of " Parsifal," the action of which is taken directly from the mysteries of the Christian religion, could not possibly be included in the regular operatic repertoire.

When I imparted this to my noble benefactor the King of Bavaria, with the most perfect understanding, he refused immediately to have the " Parsifal " given in his own Court theatre, but, on the contrary, declared that only the Festival Theatre of Bayreuth was suited to such a unique and distinct performance.

In consideration of this noble decision, it is difficult to decide as to the profitableness of publishing a piano arrangement, as an actual acquaintance with this one of my works can only be gained by a visit to the proposed yearly performance in Bayreuth for all time. . . .

## To Carl Brandt

(Bayreuth, October 17, 1881.)

*Dear Friend!*

Solicitude as to my health will not permit me to remain here much longer. On Tuesday I shall go with my family direct to Palermo (Hotel des Palmes), and expect to return only at the last moment — in May or June.

I should be anxious about this, and fear that something in connection with the next year's Festival would be neglected, did I not feel that, thanks to your care and solicitude, everything will be arranged beforehand. I feel therefore that I may put my mind quite at rest concerning the scenic and other arrangements. All musical preparation has been assumed by K. M. Levi,[1] and Dr. Schukowsky (who will also be absent from Bayreuth during the winter) has looked after all the necessary arrangements in regard to the costumes and scenic requisites; the only point

---

[1] Kapellmeister Levi.

which would cause me any uneasiness would be in the event that you, dearest colleague and friend, did not consent to act as my representative in the negotiations with the Frankfort theatrical costumier.

Therefore I beg of you to consider yourself as fully authorised by me to supervise closely the work of the costumier, to take a stand against any dilatoriness, and also to make sure of his services as chief property-man with the requisite number of assistants.

The local Executive Committee will at once support you in any measure, and Herr Gross is there to listen to any complaint.

Confident of your willingness to do this, I shall set out comforted in search of a better climate.

It is time that I should do so, for I am convinced that I shall not live another year if I remain here during the winter.

I said to Schnappauf that at most there were only five days when the sun did not shine in

Palermo, and he said it was in Upper Franconia during these five days.

Once again sincere thanks from a heart deeply grateful for your effective support in the past as well as for this my last undertaking; with you to help me I feel secure about everything — everything! With the most cordial greetings,

Yours faithfully,

RICHARD WAGNER.


To FRITZ BRANDT

(PALERMO, January 14, 1882.)

*Dear young Friend!*

Thanks for your letter — it was very kind! Not until to-day have I been able to write to you! I was obliged to postpone this distressing matter, as my condition is such that my dear wife had scruples about informing me of the sudden death of your dear father — an accident revealed to me this calamity!

You surely understand me and forgive me for not being able to put my feelings into words.

I stand in the third age of humanity, and have already seen two generations of contemporaries pass away; in your father I lost the last member of the second generation which connected me with the past.

In you I greet the third generation, to which I have surrendered the further deeds of my mature old age. I welcome you!

I assume that you are willing to carry into execution the last work in which your father and I were associated. At all events, everything is at your disposal for this, and you know exactly what is to be done in regard to the scenic production of " Parsifal."

Permit me therefore to appoint you to the position, in connection with my Bayreuth performance, made vacant by the death of your father.

During my absence of several months my Executive Council in Bayreuth will be ready to give you all information and assist you in all necessary arrangements.

To the most sympathetic greetings to your mother I add the assurances of the most friendly feeling for yourself.

Your deeply sorrowing

RICHARD WAGNER.

## TO FRIEDRICH FEUSTEL

(PALERMO, January 17, 1882.)

*My dear Friend!*

It is certainly time that I let you hear from me again! Forgive me for this neglect, but I hope that the news of me which has reached you from time to time has kept you sufficiently informed as to banish all doubts as to my loyalty and devotion.

As a matter of fact, the completion of my last great work has greatly exhausted me! Now it is finished, and may the course of its ultimate realisation present no difficulties! I shall hope so! The most unexpected interruptions, and the distressing incident of the death of my important colleague Brandt, had to be overcome.

To the son of my dead friend, Fritz, who is already thoroughly initiated into the present task, I have already transferred the completion of his father's work, and referred him to the Execu-ecutive Council in all questions concerning the same.

As for the rest, I think I have left everything in good order, so that I can feel justified in permitting myself a complete surrender to impressions so very much needed for the improvement of my bodily condition. . . .

It distresses me to see my friends in embarrassment in regard to our Festival Theatre; will you kindly convey to our excellent friend Burgomaster Muncker, first of all, my hearty thanks for his energetic stand in this not very agreeable matter.

When I take a general survey of the attitude of my own age to me during the past ten years, I must confess that the balance of my gratitude falls on the side of the friends whom I made during that time, and I herewith declare that next to my family the dearest of all things to me is *Bayreuth.*

Accept your own great and full share of this, my dearest friend, and be assured for all time of the most sincere gratitude and friendship of

Yours faithfully,

RICHARD WAGNER.

With this acknowledgment of his debt of gratitude to Bayreuth, the collection of Bayreuth Letters comes to a fitting close, but in order to carry out the " Story of Bayreuth " to its logical conclusion, it has been thought best to include the epoch-making Festival which took place in the summer of 1882.

The inception of Wagner's eleventh and last music drama of " Parsifal " must be sought in the earlier period of the composer's creative activity.

In fact, with the single exception of " Tristan and Isolde," — which, as all the world knows, was called into existence by the Swiss exile and

Wagner's friendship with Mathilde Wesendonk, — all of the music dramas were conceived at a time when their author had not yet achieved his thirty-fifth year.

In 1848 he made a sketch of a drama which was to be called " Jesus of Nazareth," and in which, for the first time, the " Parsifal " episode is foreshadowed.

That the idea in its ultimate development differed radically from the earlier sketch is to be read in the reminiscences of Frau Eliza Wille. Here this true but staunchly orthodox friend gives vehement expression to the indignation she felt at learning from Wagner that he considered the earthly love of the Magdalene for the " Prophet of Nazareth " a grateful subject for a stage work.

" He presented the ' thrilling beauty ' of this episode to us with great vivacity. I stared at him in astonishment and left the room." Later she adds: " In the last gift of his genius, in the knightly priest, *Parsifal*, and *Kundry*, who is freed from the sway of the evil spirits, is again found the idea which he already had in mind as early as 1852."

Henry T. Finck, in his Wagner biography, relates an interesting incident told him by Anton Seidl in regard to the *Flower Maiden* music. "When Seidl first became Wagner's secretary, he one day heard him playing ravishing strains, which made an indelible impression upon him. Some years later, when Seidl was putting the sketches into rough shape for practical use, Wagner played various parts for him. When he came to the *Flower Maiden* music, Seidl remarked: 'Ah, I know that!' Whereupon Wagner jumped up excitedly, almost angrily, and wanted to know where he had heard it. He was somewhat pacified on being told where, but for a long time the shock affected him, and he often said to his young secretary: 'Well, have you found any more familiar things in my music?'"

Hans von Wolzogen, the veteran Wagnerian, has quite recently put upon paper some interesting reminiscences of this " Parsifal " period, at which time he was an inmate of Wahnfried in the capacity of editor of the " Bayreuther Blätter."

" The great magician, who was usually the soul of punctuality ('tardiness,' he used to say, ' is the next thing to treason '), came in late one day to the so-called *Kindertafel*, and looking about him with a pleased smile said, ' Well, children, I have hung a mantle about my *Klingsor* to-day which I think will suit him very well.'

" Another time he gave a sigh of relief and said, ' At last I have got him off my hands, the musical-dramatic horse-radish; from now on, I shall write only quartettes.' By which we understood that he had finished the terrible *Klingsor* scene and was ready to set about giving a musical form to the *Flower Maidens*. After that we often heard the *Flower Maiden* music in the evening, which Wagner jokingly characterised as his ' latest ballet.' "

That nothing was further from Wagner's

thought than any set of terpsichorean evolutions
borrowed from the operatic stage, for which he
had so profound a contempt, was proven by his
letter inviting Richard Fricke to come to Bayreuth and assume direction of the *Flower Maiden*
scene, " which is to be absolutely un-ballet like.
I can show you what I mean! Your material
will be: soloists of the best quality, at their head
the Lehmann sisters," to which Fricke responded,
" Give me a sufficient number of Lilli Lehmanns
and I could tear the world to pieces."

Fricke was the Nestor among the German
dancing-masters of that period, but he cared less
for the technique of the ballet than the artistic
thought and the true spirit of the composition.
He was a thinking artist, and it was this rare
quality which attracted and held the interest of
such a man as Richard Wagner.

It was Fricke who was called to Bayreuth in
1875 to organise the horde of the *Nibelung* in
their comically drastic motions, and it was he
who was again summoned when the *Flower*

*Maidens* were to be trained in their difficult evolutions.

In this connection it is of interest to read a characteristic effusion which was sent to Lilli Lehmann in response to her request to be allowed to see the score of the music:

"Oh, my best of all the Lillis! To let the 'Parsifal' score go out of my hands requires serious consideration. The composition is finished, and anyone who comes to me here in Bayreuth can hear it played from beginning to end by Rubinstein (Josef).

"But — as I said — first I must consider it a little.

"But my *Kapellmeisterin* Lilli shall see what she now has to do! All sorts of devilish ideas which only occurred to me because her genius was ever before me. Without Lilli is *Klingsor's* sorcery not to be accomplished.

"Oh, and here she has something to sing! If she would only come, she could see it; she must be responsible for the entire thing! But — to send it away — out of the house, that is impossible just now. What an unlucky star could hang over such a manuscript!

" Therefore — we must act together!"

In a later letter Wagner writes: " Here is a sort of piano arrangement of the scene with the *Flower Maidens* in the second act of ' Parsifal.' Take a close look at it; it is no joke, and from this single scene you will be able to see that my latest work is not intended for the theatres scattered here and there and everywhere." [1]

Hans von Wolzogen was also one of the little band who listened to the " Parsifal " drama at Wahnfried in September, 1877, the occasion being the Conference of the Delegates.

" This reading was my first experience in Wahnfried! And what a memorable event it was to me! Think of hearing the ' Parsifal ' drama for the very first time (without an inkling

---

[1] This letter is from the recently published volume of correspondence, "Richard Wagner to His Artists," and appears here, for the first time in English, by the courtesy of the German publishers, Schuster & Loeffler (Berlin).

of it more than the hint given me by Emil Heckel that there was a sort of Venusberg scene!) and to become acquainted with it out of the poet's own mouth!

"His delivery was characterised by the greatest degree of naturalness, without any attempt at pathos, and was only raised to the ethical power of expression by the emotional sincerity of its creator! Here, for the first time, *Gurnemanz* and the young knights were awakened by the morning call from the Grailsberg; here for the first time appeared the enigmatic figure of *Kundry*, the wild messenger of the Grail; here for the first time the sick king was borne in with impressive solemnity; here for the first time we heard the expression 'pure fool' and saw the mysterious picture of the sacred spear!

'O wunden, wundervoller heiliger Speer!'

Not even when heard in Scaria's most powerful tones did this invocation of the mysterious symbol affect me as strangely as in this reading of the Master's. I remember that all of these strange and surprising occurrences, which followed each other in such quick succession, impressed me at first as a romantic epic of adventure, with an uncanny mysterious meaning, and it was not until the second act that I awoke from this epic dream and began to grasp the real meaning of the drama — the great drama of redemption: *Parsifal — Kundry!*"

Franz Liszt, ever the high-minded champion of the Bayreuth Master, wrote:

"The sketch of 'Parsifal,' which Wagner read to us recently, is filled and permeated with the essence of Christianity. It would be a singular inconsistency to admire the last scene of 'Faust' (Part Second) and to condemn 'Parsifal,' which, to me, seems to stand on the same plane of mystic inspiration. In fact, I am willing to confess that most of our poets who are regarded as Christian-Catholics stand far behind Wagner in their religious sentiments."

Reference has already been made to the musical surprise prepared by Wagner for his wife Cosima in Triebschen, December 25, 1870, when he made her a birthday present of the " Siegfried Idyll."

The same date, eight years later, was chosen as a christening day for the " Parsifal Vorspiel." In chronicling this event Glasenapp says:

" Through the generosity of the Duke of Meiningen the ducal orchestra was granted a two days' leave of absence, and placed at Wagner's disposal for the first performance of the ' Parsifal Vorspiel,' which took place in the hall at Wahnfried between seven and eight in the morning. The impression created by the sublime sounds, heard here for the first time, was an indescribable one. . . . It was the birthday of the ' Parsifal Vorspiel,' the most sublime orchestral prelude ever presented to the musical world."

Two months before, Wagner had written a letter to his friend, Edward Dannreuther, in London, the chief burden of which was a request

that some Yorkshire hams be sent him, and closing with the remark, " The ' Vorspiel ' is finished.  It sounds very nice! "

It was Dannreuther to whom a second appeal
of a totally different nature was sent two years
later, in reference to the bells whose solemn peal-
ing closes the first and last acts.  According to
Henry T. Finck these bells unfortunately were
a failure at the first " Parsifal " Festival.  Their
sound was to be produced by a kind of specially
constructed hammer-klavier.  At later festivals a
great improvement was effected by combining the
sounds of tam-tams with the piano strings; " but
absolute illusion has not yet been reached in this
respect."

Wagner himself realised the inadequacy of the
first attempt, and hence his telegram to Dannreuther four days preceding the first performance :

" My kingdom for a tam-tam!  With the
proper C normal Diapason! "

The response with which the " Parsifal " idea

met gave a strong impetus to the work, and succeeded in effectively dispelling from Wagner's mind the whimsical idea to which he gave expression in one of his moments of despondency.

"When my old friend *Brunnhilde* leaps into the funeral pyre, I shall also rush into the flames, and hope to find there a blessed death. So that is settled! Amen!"

He felt impelled to give a new — perhaps a last — musical message to the world, and the musical sketches for the "Parsifal" score grew with astonishing rapidity.

"Parsifal" had been promised for the summer of 1880, and could have been easily completed had the enthusiasm of the intimate circle of friends in and about Wahnfried, who were following with such intense interest every step in the development of this music-drama, communicated itself to the German public at large.

But this was not the case, and at a meeting of the Society of Patrons at Wiesbaden in March,

1880, there was no alternative but that of postponing the " Parsifal " Festival until 1882.

Wagner was at the time in Palermo, endeavouring to regain his health and enjoy the absolute rest and quiet necessary to the completion of his " Parsifal," and it was at the Hotel des Palmes in Palermo that (January 13, 1882) he could write the word *Finis* on the score. But before this auspicious point had been reached, he was forced to pass through another slough of despondency, and in his disgust at the complete indifference of the German nation, he seriously contemplated moving to America.

To Hans von Wolzogen he wrote at this time: " . . . I hope to be able to stand it in my native land, and am ready for anything if — yes, if? — Dearest friend, I shall leave off for to-day with this 'if,' for it makes me too sad to give expression to my absolute hopelessness concerning European, and more especially German, culture.

" This firm conviction of its ever-increasing decadence is so strong in me that, in order to preserve the seed which I possess, I have seriously thought of a complete and permanent removal to America, in order to plant this seed when it will fructify in a soil composed of German elements."

Again it was King Ludwig who removed the difficulties which threatened to obstruct the realisation of the second Bayreuth Festival. After listening to the " Parsifal Vorspiel," played by his own orchestra under the bâton of the composer, he consented to assume the protectorate of the Festival, at the same time placing at Wagner's disposal the forces of the Munich Opera under the joint conductors Hermann Levi and Franz Fischer.

Without this intervention of the King, Wagner's last artistic deed could not have been carried to its execution — at least, not without a repetition of the unpleasant features of the first Festival, and an involving of the enterprise in renewed financial confusion.

The appointment of Hermann Levi as the

musical director of " Parsifal" led to an anonymous letter being sent to Wagner, in which he was implored "to keep his work undefiled and not let it be conducted by a Jew." Wagner, who did not take the matter at all seriously, showed the letter to Levi, who, fearful of further misunderstandings and unpleasantnesses, took an unceremonious departure from Bayreuth, but was recalled *en route* by a telegram and a letter begging him "to pay no attention to such nonsense, but for Heaven's sake come back and get really acquainted with us. . . . This may, perhaps, mean an entire change in your life but — in any case — you are my ' Parsifal ' conductor."

And again: " You are my plenipotentiary, my *alter ego* for the ' Parsifal ' performances next year!"

One of the young musicians who had allied himself to the Wagnerian cause was Engelbert Humperdinck, who was chosen to perform the duties of an itinerant coach and was sent about from place to place to take the singers through their preliminary studies in the " Parsifal " score. Wagner, according to a well-known fashion of his, allowed himself many liberties with Humperdinck's name, writing once to Levi:

" The six solo Magic Maidens are to be coached by Humperting! . . . Have you a score? If not, you can get one from Hump!"

The preliminary rehearsals for " Parsifal " took place in the summer of 1881, but as only one work was to be gotten ready for this second Festival, instead of the four composing the mammoth musical structure of the " Ring," a month was deemed sufficient.

Moreover, during the six years that had elapsed since the first Festival, a nucleus of competent artists had been formed, so that the casting of the various *rôles* did not cause the same trouble as in 1876; in fact, there was no difficulty in securing three casts.

Winkelmann, Jäger, and Gudehus were cast for the *Parsifal;* Materna, Marianne Brandt, and Therese Malten were to alternate in singing the

*Kundry; Gurnemanz* by Emil Scaria and Siehr;
*Amfortas*, Reichmann and Beck; *Titurel*, Kin-
dermann; *Klingsor*, Hill and Fuchs; and Lilli
Lehmann as the leader of the *Flower Maidens*.
The chorus was composed of eighty-four voices,
and in addition a boys' chorus of fifty voices;
the orchestra, under Hermann Levi, was composed of a hundred and five players, of whom
seventy-three came from the Royal Opera in
Munich.

Since then the physiognomy of musical Germany has gone through material modifications.
Munich no more sends the nucleus of the orchestra and chorus, as the increase in home consump-
tion resulting from the inauguration of its own
Wagner Festival has prevented this exportation.

Instead of this, Berlin, one of the last cities
to recognise ungrudgingly the greatness of the
living Wagner, does honour to the dead Prophet
by supplying the larger part of the Festival *personnel*. Dr. Karl Muck has succeeded Hermann
Levi as the "'Parsifal' plenipotentiary," and

it is usually the fresh young voices from the Court Church in Berlin which ring out so pure and true from the cupola of the Grail Temple.

Winkelmann, the creator of the *Parsifal*, who has just died in Vienna at the age of sixty-three, in some rather recent reminiscences of the " Parsifal " period, creates a very vivid picture of Wagner's magnetic influence upon his artists:

" Anton Seidl, who was at that time (1881) musical director in Leipzig, brought about a meeting between Wagner and myself. Once when I was singing in Leipzig, he asked if I would have the courage to sing *Parsifal* in Bayreuth. The Festival was then in course of preparation. After some consideration I said I would, and we travelled together to the Mecca of the Prophet.

" Wagner immediately exercised an overpowering effect upon me. I can see him standing before me, can see every gesture, his facial expression, his tremendous enthusiasm for the cause which he believed to be a holy one. I can hear

his voice as he spoke to me long and convincingly, and asked me if 'on my word of honour'
I really felt that I possessed the strength necessary for the *Parsifal*.

"And then he explained to me, for hours at
a time, the content of his work, the significance
of each single character, of every scene, and
showed me the connection between it all.

"Richard Wagner was of a truth a genuine
revelation for the artists who at that time had
not yet been able to emancipate themselves from
the 'farce' of expressing themselves by mean-
ingless poses and musical violence.

"How entirely different was Wagner's authority over us; he was not contented to be
merely our musical director and stage manager,
but was our adviser and teacher! Wagner hated
every pose on the stage, any straining after effect, every disturbing movement.

"He used to say: 'the acting must be con-
trolled by the *intelligence!*' 'Everything must
be genuine, sincere, on the stage.'

" 'Do you think you are in a theatre!' he cried to a singer who was making the most impossible gesticulations. 'Those are swimming exercises, no human gestures! Anyone who is *unnatural*, I consider as my enemy!' These were some of his dicta from the 'Parsifal' rehearsals . . . What iron nerves, what incredible energy, what burning enthusiasm! That was a glorious period!"

One of the most interesting pictures of the " Parsifal " period is " An Evening in the Wahnfried," representing Wagner in the midst of a select circle of enthusiasts.

The Festival was on a firmer financial basis, thanks to Hans von Bülow's generous gift of forty thousand marks and another ten thousand from Friedrich Schön of Worms; and Wagner's own contribution, leaving quite out of the question his gift of a priceless musical legacy, was the sum of sixty thousand marks, the amount paid for the " Parsifal " score by the publishing firm of Schott and Sons in Mayence.

The first " Parsifal " Festival took place in the summer of 1882 (July 26–August 29), and in spite of the religious character of the content which departed so radically from the previous trend of the Wagnerian dramas, there was an extraordinary manifestation of interest in the work, and the impression created by it was a strong and lasting one.

This new revelation of a supreme poetic and musical genius, together with the magic of the mystic consecration, took powerful hold upon the listeners, and never before nor since has a theatre been the scene of such rare and genuine emotion.

Tappert writes: " A nobler and more beautiful legacy than this *Bühnenweihfestspiel* could not have been left us by the Master. In the temple of the Holy Grail we were all moved to hold out our hands in reconciliation, to whatever religious sect we belonged."

It was the second time that Wagner's patrons and disciples had rallied around him in Bayreuth.

Was he, perhaps, moved by a strange presentiment, when during the last performance he seized the bâton in the third act and directed his swan song to its close?

" Parsifal " was presented under quite different circumstances from the ill-fated " Ring "! Fourteen performances for a paying public had placed it on a firm material basis; the receipts exceeded all expectations, and covered not only all expenses, but left a balance of six thousand marks, so that the reserve fund of fourteen thousand marks remained untouched.

With confidence the Society of Patrons could make their Festival plans for the following and succeeding years, and the composer could look on with a hitherto unknown degree of artistic assurance, and a blessed freedom from financial anxiety.

The fate of the Bayreuth Festival was assured, but the creator of the Festival was not to live to enjoy his triumph.

A few months after the white dove had hov-

ered over the head of " Parsifal," another messenger, this time a sable-hued one, entered the
Palazzo Vendramin in Venice and on February
13, 1883, the news flashed around the world:
"*Richard Wagner is dead!*"

He was laid to rest in the garden of his beloved Wahnfried, and no pilgrim to Bayreuth
fails to pay a visit of reverent homage to the
last resting-place of the Master of Bayreuth.

Richard Wagner needs no epitaph, for by his
works he is known, least of all by the Epitaphium
which he wrote in a moment of bitter sarcasm
in the year 1864, just when the horizon of his
art was hung so heavy with clouds, and he had
no prophetic feeling that the " German Prince "
whom he had invoked had been found, and was
about to send out his messenger in all directions
to search for the great and lonely composer and
bring him to his court.

Just before the clouds lifted, Wagner wrote
this earlier epitaph (only recently published)
which ran as follows:

" Hier liegt Wagner, der nichts geworden
Nicht einmal Ritter vom humpigen Orden;
Nicht einen Hund hintern Ofen entlockt er,
Universitäten nicht'mal 'nen Dockter!"

That the idea outlived its creator is a proof
not only of the essential greatness of the art
work itself, but of the growing intelligence of the
German public and the world at large to accept
the work of a reformer when the reformer himself was dead and gone.

The legal copyright of the work expires in
1913, but an effort is being made by the friends
of the Wagnerian music drama to have this
period extended by a special act of the Imperial
Parliament.

Should this measure eventually be carried, it
would be convincing proof that Germany knows
how to respect the musical legacy left her by the
greatest and most genuinely German composer.

It would however be erroneous to convey the
impression that the family at Wahnfried and the
friends of the Wagnerian art have set their hearts
and hopes upon effecting a change in the Ger-

man copyright laws, which should serve only the interests of the Wagnerian music dramas. On the contrary, the effort is being made to have the author's copyright in general extended from thirty to fifty years, and thus avoid the frequent friction arising out of the dissimilarity between the German and French laws — as in France an author's works are already protected for fifty years after his death.

The fact that a large party in Germany is strongly opposed to violating the express wish of the creator of "Parsifal" leads to the general belief that, even should the copyright not be extended, no German stage of any repute would venture to defy the public opinion to the extent of including "Parsifal" in its heterogeneous repertory.

Wagner at many times and in many places expressed himself in terms not to be misunderstood concerning the disposition of his last stage work, but never more convincingly than in a letter written to his noble friend and pa-

tron, King Ludwig of Bavaria, written from
Siena,

" Having been obliged to surrender all of my
works so ideally conceived to the theatres and
to a public which I deem so deeply ill suited for
such a work, I now ask myself the serious question, whether I should not at least preserve this
last and most sacred of my works from the fate
of being doomed to an ordinary operatic career.

" In the mere content and character of ' Parsifal,' I recognise the imperative necessity for
no longer disregarding such a decision.  In fact,
how can an action, into which the most sublime mysteries of the Christian faith are introduced, be presented in theatres like ours, be
closely associated with our customary operatic
repertoire, and be given before such a public as
assembles there?  I should really not blame our
church committees if they took a firm stand
against the presentation of the most consecrated
mysteries on the stage upon which yesterday and
to-morrow frivolity comfortably disports itself,

and before a public attracted solely by such frivolity.

"Imbued by the spirit, I called my ' Parsifal ' a *Buhnenweihfestspiel*, ' a Festival Play for the Consecration of the Stage.'

" I must therefore endeavour to consecrate a stage to this work, and this can only be my isolated stage Festival House in Bayreuth.

" There the ' Parsifal ' is to be given for all time and there only; *never* is the ' Parsifal ' to be presented in any other theatre, nor offered any audience as a mere diversion." [1]

A book purporting to deal with the historical and artistic development of the Bayreuth Idea is not the proper place for an ethical discussion of the " Parsifal " question in its relation to other stages and other audiences from those for which it was originally designed. And yet the writer cannot refrain from quoting a passage from Wolfgang Golther's little book on Bayreuth, as

[1] This letter is from the volume "Richard Wagner to His Friends and Contemporaries," and appears here by the courtesy of the German publishers, Schuster & Loeffler (Berlin).

it so admirably and concisely expresses the German attitude toward any disturbance of Wagner's original plan.  Golther has this to say: "The American theft of the *grail*, and the expiration of the copyright of this sacred work, must be deplored both from artistic as well as moral reasons.  The release of the 'Parsifal' rights is unworthy chaffering with something that is holy, a profanation of our deepest and tenderest religious sentiments, a source of endless errors and misunderstandings, a misinterpretation of the purest principles of art, a sin against the Holy Ghost of German art, and an act of the greatest irreverence against the last wish of our great Master."

# INDEX

Duke of Nassau, 153

Eilers, Albert, 197
Eliot, George, 284, 287
Erlanger, Baron Emile, 125-126
Erlanger, Baron Viktor von, 148
Essex, 286

Feustel, Frau, 318n
Feustel, Friedrich, 13-14, 44, 54, 59-60, 156, 170, 177, 232, 233n,
    237, 244-245, 259, 277, 289, 301; letters from Richard Wagner,
    12, 17-18, 28-33, 36-37, 42-43, 46-52, 55-57, 62-64, 69-78, 78-89,
    99-100, 102-103, 109-110, 119-123, 125-127, 130-131, 135-136,
    162-167, 177-178, 184-185, 199-201, 205-210, 219-220, 230-233,
    252-259, 265-276, 289-305, 308-310, 318-322, 327-330, 335-337
Finck, Henry Theophilus, *Wagner and His Works,* 25n, 97n; 168,
    258, 287, 339, 347
Fischer, 231
Fischer, Franz, 178, 223, 232, 313-314, 350
Franck, 78
Frederick II (the Great) of Prussia, 99
Fricke, Richard, 196n, 223-224, 341-342
Friedrich I, Grand Duke of Baden, 117, 121, 152-53, 156
Friedrich, (Margrave), 99
Friedrich Franz II, Grand Duke of Mecklenburg, 153
Fuchs, 353

Georg II, Duke of Meiningen, 346
Glasenapp, Carl Friedrich, *Life of Richard Wagner,* 13-14; 114, 219,
    346
Goethe, Johann Wolfgang von, 1, 263-264; *Faust,* 345
Golther, Wolfgang, 363-364
Grand Duke of Saxon Weimar, 153
Grant, Ulysses Simpson, 304
Gross, Adolph, 233, 244, 252, 289, 292, 298, 321, 332
Gudehus, Heinrich, 352

Hanlein, 54n
Heckel, Emil, 15, 23-24, 54n, 112, 120, 135, 141, 143, 155-158, 194,
    218, 231n, 232, 245, 261, 266, 277, 303-304, 326n, 344; letters
    from Richard Wagner, 22, 27-28, 33-36, 54-55, 60-62, 101-102,